Fundamentals of Parliamentary Debate: Approaches for the 21st Century

Second Edition

Michael H. Eaves

Carl M. Cates

Daniel E. Schabot

Valdosta State University

Kendall Hunt
publishing company

Cover image © Shutterstock, Inc.

Kendall Hunt
publishing company

www.kendallhunt.com
Send all inquiries to:
4050 Westmark Drive
Dubuque, IA 52004-1840

Copyright © 2004, 2010 by Michael H. Eaves, Carl M. Cates and Dan E. Schabot

ISBN 978-0-7575-7121-3

Printed in the United States of America
10 9 8 7 6 5 4 3 2 1

Contents

Chapter 1

A Brief History of Parliamentary Debate

Key Terms

NDT   APDA
CEDA   NPDA

T here are several different styles of intercollegiate debate in the United
States. In turn, there are variations in practice, terminology, and rules in
intercollegiate debate. This text serves as an introduction to parliamentary debate. As part of that introduction, a short history of intercollegiate
debate as a whole is offered. Debate is an educational activity as well as a
competitive one. Different forms of debate simply offer students a multitude
of ways of learning through debating.

INTERCOLLEGIATE DEBATE

For years, intercollegiate debate involved schools competing one on one against other schools. Schools would send participants from their debate or forensics society for the competitions. Eaves (2006) uncovered and analyzed a debate between the University of Florida and the University of Tennessee from 1918. Much like many debates of today, debaters argued over a public policy issue that was important at the time.

The debaters had to defend or reject a proposition. Propositions are statements that advocate an idea or action for the purpose of academic argument. For example, a debater in the 1930s might have debated the proposition that FDR should abandon new deal policies. The proposition, in this case, would advocate government policy change. The opposition team would argue that FDR's new deal policy is sound and should not be abandoned.

The movie *The Great Debaters* showed a fictionalized version of early intercollegiate debate. The movie did an excellent job showing that debaters had to do a great deal of research to support their arguments. However, the use of personal examples in the movie to win debates was not and is not a common practice in debate. Debaters won debates by using evidence and documented examples to support their arguments.

Shuuterstock © Melinda fauver. Under the licence from shutterstock, inc.

University of Tennessee pictured here.

EVIDENTIARY DEBATE

The National Debate Tournament (NDT) was established in 1947 and held at the United States Military Academy at West Point (An Introduction to the National Debate Tournament, 2009). In the decade leading up to the NDT, it was not uncommon for several schools to gather together on one campus and debate each other. After the NDT was formed, tournament-style debate was the predominate form of debate in the country. A tournament consists of preliminary and elimination rounds. Teams of two people debate each other in the preliminary round and obtain a win–loss record. Teams with the best records then participate in a single elimination bracketed tournament. The NDT format was the model used by many intercollegiate tournaments.

While some organizations had yearlong topics before the NDT, a change for most debating societies was a single-year topic. Schools that participated in the NDT debated the same topic for the entire year. The topics were always policy propositions. Thus, NDT debate is often known as policy debate. The debate teams were required to gather a lot of evidence on a single issue. By the time the NDT took place every year, teams had hundreds of pieces of evidence supporting their positions. In NDT debate, one's ability to conduct research was equal to one's ability to speak.

The emphasis placed on research resulted in a rapid style of delivery that many competitors and coaches did not desire. The emphasis on research led to the use of many technical terms for American collegiate debate, which you will learn later in this text. Jones (1978) summarized the discontent with the NDT as one that revolved around "rapid-fire delivery, heavy reliance on evidence cards, and squirrel cases . . ." As a result of the discontent, the Cross Examination Debate Association (CEDA) was founded in 1971 (Cross Examination Debate Association, 2008).

CEDA offered propositions that dealt with changing values instead of changing policies. There were also two topics per year to deemphasize the reliance on evidence. However, CEDA eventually changed their policies and in 1996 began using the same yearlong topic that the NDT used. Today, while both organizations function separately, a team can enter an NDT-sanctioned tournament and a CEDA-sanctioned tournament and expect to see a similar style of debate.

Other organizations in the United States offer evidence-based debate. The National Educational Debate Association (NEDA) and its eventual short-lived spin-off the Great Plains Forensics Conference left CEDA at around the same time it combined with NDT. NEDA was concerned with the same issues as the CEDA originally was. In their Objectives and Procedures

(National Debate Educational Association, 2005), it states: "debate should be a practical educational experience and that performance by participants should reflect the stylistic and analytical skill . . ." The National Forensics Association also offers Lincoln–Douglas-style (one on one) policy debate with a new topic each year.

PARLIAMENTARY DEBATE

Parliamentary debate was popular in the United Kingdom, Ireland, and other parts of Europe long before it became popular here. International parliamentary debating began in the early twentieth century including teams from Oxford University touring the United States (Flynn, 2002). Louisiana State University also hosted a parliamentary debate tournament for several years before a formalized organization was created (Peterson, 1982).

The Transatlantic University Speech Association attempted to bring together English speaking countries for tournaments in the 1970s (American Parliamentary Debate Association, 2009; Flynn, 2002). The first world debating competition took place in 1981 (Flynn, 2002). At the same time, a group of about 15 universities in the Northeast formed the American Parliamentary Debate Association (APDA) (A Brief History of the APDA, 2009). The organization was formalized as a nonprofit organization in 1999.

While the APDA was unique to the Northeast, the rest of the country was still participating in evidentiary debate. Many schools had the same problem with both CEDA and NDT as they had when CEDA was originally formed (Horn, 1994). Specifically, programs cited problems with speed of delivery, reemergence of squirrel cases, and counterplans (Horn, 1994; Stanfield and West, 1995). Several tournaments in the 1990s experimented with divisions of evidentiary debate that emphasized delivery.

As a response to some of these issues, some debate programs in the Western United States began experimenting with parliamentary debate (Johnson, Johnson, & Trapp, 1999). Some programs felt that evidentiary debate was inaccessible to beginning debaters. They used parliamentary debate to train debaters so that they could compete in evidence-based debate later on. Al Johnson, of Colorado College, and Major Gwendolyn Fayne, of the United States Air Force Academy, offered a parliamentary division at a tournament in the fall of 1991. After two other parliamentary tournaments that year, the Rocky Mountain Championship was organized. By the spring of 1993, the organization expanded and changed its name to the National Parliamentary Debate Association (NPDA). Today, the NPDA is the single largest collegiate debate association in the United States.

Another organization, the International Public Debate Association (IPDA), formed in 1997 (Cirlin, 1999). Public debate was created to help programs in the Southern United States transition away from evidentiary debate. Despite efforts to expand, IPDA has had difficulty establishing itself as an organization outside of the South.

In recent years, differences of opinion have once again surfaced in the American debate community. The National Parliamentary Tournament of Excellence (NPTE) was launched in 2001. The NPTE requires teams to qualify for the tournament based on their record throughout the year. In 2009, NPTE took steps to formalize itself as an independent organization. However, NPDA and NPTE often sanction the same tournaments.

Characteristics of Parliamentary-Style Debate

There are some features that APDA, NPDA, NPTE, and IPDA all have in common. Instead of having a yearlong or semiyearly proposition, a new proposition is used every round. Debaters are not allowed to read directly from any evidentiary source during the round. Debaters are not given preparation time during the round. Instead, they use anywhere from 15 minutes to 30 minutes to prepare for the proposition they receive. APDA, NPDA, and NPTE have debaters debate in two-person teams. IPDA uses Lincoln–Douglas-style, one-on-one debate.

In general, three types of propositions—fact, value, and policy—were used in tournaments. A discussion of the different types of resolution is offered in Chapter 6. There has been a push in some parts of the NPDA and NPTE community to eliminate fact and value propositions. Some tournaments have also started to offer topic areas. The idea is that students will have better debates because they can develop arguments for topic areas before they arrive at the tournament. Regardless of the philosophy of a debater, a coach, a program, or an organization, parliamentary-style debate is the most practiced style of intercollegiate debate in the United States. This text will provide some insight into developing skills for NPDA-style debate. However, many of these skills could be used in any form of parliamentary-style debate.

REFERENCES

American Parliamentary Debate Association. (2009). A brief history of APDA. Retrieved May 24, 2009, from http://www.apdaweb.org/about/history

Cirlin, A. (1999). The origins of the IPDA. Retrieved May 24, 2009, from http://www.ipdadebate.org/mission.html

Cross Examination Debate Association. (2008). About CEDA. Retrieved May 24, 2009, from http://www.cedadebate.org/?q=about

Eaves, M. (2006). *A rhetorical analysis of the 1918 debate between the University of Florida and the University of Tennessee.* Paper presented at the 76th Annual Southern States Communication Association Convention. Dallas, TX.

Flynn, C. (2002). History of the World Debating Championships. Retrieved May 24, 2009, from http://flynn.debating.net/worhist.htm

Horn, G. (1994). *Why are programs leaving CEDA?* Paper presented at the 80th Annual Meeting of the Speech Communication Association. New Orleans. ERIC document reproduction service no. ED 377531. http://www.edrs.com/default.cfm

Johnson, A., Johnson, S., & Trapp, R. (1999). An early history of parliamentary debate. Retrieved May 24, 2009, from *http://www.parlidebate.org /history/an-early-history-of-the-npda/*

Jones, M. A. (1978). CEDA vs. NDT: the fact-value dichotomy emerges in educational debate. Position paper, Conway, Arkansas. ERIC document reproduction service no. ED 203396. http://www.edrs.com/default.cfm

National Debate Tournament. (2009). An introduction to the National Debate Tournament. Retrieved May 24, 2009, from http://groups.wfu.edu/NDT/Articles/ndtintro.html

National Debate Educational Association. (2005). NEDA objectives and procedures. Retrieved May 24, 2009, from http://neda.us/index.php?option=com_content&task=view&id=15&Itemid=2

Peterson, O. (1982). Forum debating: 150 debates later. *Southern Communication Journal, 47* (Summer), 435–443.

Stanfield, S., & West, I. (1995). *Counterplans: the evolution of negative burdens as CEDA makes the transition from value to policy debate.* Paper presented at the 81st Annual Meeting of the Speech Communication Association, San Antonio. ERIC document reproduction service no. ED 314771. http://www.edrs.com/default.cfm

Chapter 2

Delivery, Language, and Humor

Key Terms

VOLUME   PITCH
SPEED   ARTICULATION
GESTURES   EYE CONTACT
BODY MOVEMENT   HECKLING

One of the biggest assets of training in parliamentary debate is its connection to speaking in professional contexts. As pointed out in the chapter on history, one of the distinguishing marks of parliamentary debate is its dedication to clarity rather than speed. Few audiences can follow the speed of delivery common to policy debate but instead would be drawn by comparison to the type of delivery praised by both the ancients and current consumers of oratory. The purpose of this chapter is to discuss good delivery, language choice, and appropriate use of humor.

DELIVERY

The same characteristics that are judged successful in public speaking must be considered in parliamentary debate. Vocal attributes such as volume, pitch, speed, articulation, and pauses should be used as tools. Nonverbal characteristics such as gestures, posture, eye contact, and stage movements are just as important. The attitude connotated by these combinations is central to your success.

Vocal Attributes

It is an old adage that how you say something is as important as what you say. A few years ago, the second author (C.M.C.) witnessed a student's speech that had dazzling content. Her work with visual aids was groundbreaking for its day, and the support materials were sterling. A few moments into the speech, the student started with awkward interjections into the speech with ums and uhs. A somewhat bored student started keeping count and told me later that he had counted nearly three hundred verbal breakers. This poor demonstration of delivery skill destroyed her hard work by rendering the speech as ineffective and as an oral train wreck for her audience. Skills with which one wields the spoken work are no less important to the debater.

Volume may seem a small concern in the classrooms or competition rooms of debate. After all, how many people are usually present in a round? Although few good debaters have trouble being heard, this issue is still worth considering. Obviously, the debater must speak at a level to be audible to judges and audience alike, but of more importance is the use of the voice to accentuate the message. This is more than avoiding monotone. The proper use of volume can serve to accentuate the argument. Reducing volume can serve to emphasize a point just as well if not better than yelling. Emphasis on a critical element of the speech may need an elevated level to push by heckling. However, you never wish to be perceived as yelling at the audience or the judge. Volume is a tool to emphasize the message and not to attack the room or its attendees. The second author recalls judging a team years ago from a south central state in a policy debate. He felt as though he had been assaulted by the duo. All speakers were loud and cross-examinations were nearly screamed. He felt as abused as the opposing squad did.

Pitch is another vocal attribute to give attention to. A few years ago, I had a marvelous student with one of the most distinctly unusual voices I have heard. When in class, her nasal, shrill, and drawl-filled voice could set her classmates into an eye-rolling frenzy. Imagine what it did to her debate audience. It was difficult to get past her voice to hear the merit of her argument. After she took a course in voice and diction, she could vary her pitch and control her drawl to ease the burden on her audience. Speaking in any pitch without variation can ruin your effort. While you do not wish to sound like a calliope, your skilled variations in pitch can enhance the receipt of your speech for judges and audience alike.

Speech rate influences both the credibility and legibility of your speeches. While variation is important here , especially for emphasis, the parliamentary debater needs to be especially aware of the history of speed in speaking as it relates to this activity. Historically in policy debate, it has been critical to introduce or counter as much evidence into a round as physically possible. A faster rate of speech allows more to be spoken. Although this is appropriate for a competition with a trained judge with special knowledge, it is a poor translation of oral skills for the general audience and the working world. Parliamentary debate, while still constrained by time, allows the speaker to clearly introduce arguments rather than depend on the speed of the judges' ear. Clarity is critical. This does not mean that you must speak slowly. You should find an appropriate speech rate that is natural to your style, while at the same time being cognizant of the judge's reaction during the debate. The speech rate in parliamentary debate has increased in recent years and has changed to a fast conversational style. This rate is common in the varsity divisions at tournaments, whereas novice-level competition typically enjoys slower speech rates from those competitors.

In addition, articulation affects credibility. As someone who has coached speakers and taught classes for more than twenty years, this writer knows the disastrous consequences to credibility if words are spoken incorrectly. It makes the speaker look uninformed if not poorly educated. I never understood in my elementary and junior high years why my father would make me look up terms in the dictionary and figure out how to say the term according to the pronunciation guides. I do now. Further, with web resources offering audio pronunciation links, no debater should ever be in error.

In an activity where time is so critical, how can you afford time for pauses? Good parliamentary speaking can benefit from the well-placed pause for effect. However, do not let it drag or you may open yourself to heckles of others. For example, do not use the rhetorical question and then pause for drama. It opens the heckling door for a good comeback by your opponents. If you use pauses, do not be so long as to lose control of the speech.

Nonverbal Characteristics

Students of communication know the importance of nonverbal components of speaking (Leathers & Eaves, 2008). How you visually communicate with the

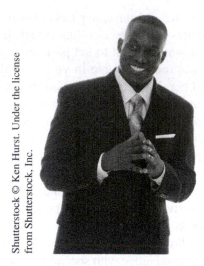

Shutterstock © Ken Hurst. Under the license from Shutterstock, Inc.

judge and audience can put you over the top, if managed well. How to dress is not covered here because styles change and competitions may have individual rules.

Consider the following real life example about a student and a speech assignment. A young man was incredibly enthusiastic about the assignment, a speech in which they were to use a visual aid to describe themselves to the class. He was however incredibly nervous. After conferring with well-intentioned friends and family, he was advised to move his arms and breathe after each main point. During his speech, this translated into him raising his arms after most sentences and exhaling loudly. Over the course of the five minutes, he took on the appearance of a large bird unsuccessfully trying to leave the nest. No one remembered what he said, but they all remembered his gestures.

Gestures properly handled are necessary tools to emphasize and complement your arguments. Use hand movements that make sense, not movements that look choppy or artificial. You want to make your hands part of your message, not the message. One of my professors from graduate school who had taught debate after World War Two used to bemoan the loss of scripted, choreographed speeches for debate. Part of his chagrin was the loss of impact to the speeches in the rounds due to the loss of emphasis contributed by well-planned gestures. Conversely, keep those hands out of your pockets. We do not really want to speculate what is happening there! If you cannot find any other use for your hands, rest your hands on the lectern.

Good posture can aid your message. Slumping, slouching, or dragging your body along does not bespeak of confidence. This does not mean that you have to take on a cotillion look, but you need to portray confidence. Slumping over the podium like a crutch makes it appear as if it is your crutch. Slouching makes you look like a victim. Stand up! Appear confident based on your stance! Unlike policy debate, parliamentary debate places a real premium on the effectiveness of a speaker's posture in the speech. While some debaters do ask questions from a sitting position, it is generally frowned upon, and standing while one speaks is all but required.

Problems with posture usually connect to problems with eye contact. If you are looking at the floor because of posture, then you are likely to be looking at the floor when you are speaking. In our society, much of credibility and believability is tied to eye contact. While we talk of cultural differences, content issues, and general critical thinking, no wise speaker intentionally places barriers to success with an audience. Poor eye contact is a barrier. It makes people question your veracity and reliability. Make eye contact with the judge. Connect with the judge. If you are speaking with a significant audience, then select people around the room and make eye contact with them. This will make people feel that you have made eye contact with them. It is critical however, that you do not make eye contact with your opponents. This longstanding tradition in debate, if violated, would make you appear crude and uneducated during the activity.

While it is common for debaters in parliamentary debate to move while speaking, stage movement must be used for effect and not as revelation of a nervous tic. While the comparison is imperfect because the students were in a public speaking class, this story serves as a great illustration. The student was speaking regarding his training techniques as a bull rider on the rodeo circuit. He had done a commendable amount of preparation with a board diagram, scale model, and props. These were placed in the front of the room at three different stations. At first the second author (C.M.C.) thought his skipping to station one was, however cheesy, an attention-getting device,

but when he was playing the air guitar, hopping on one foot to station two, to the howls of the class, the second author began to wonder if he was impaired. He had no recollection of doing either, even when confronted with videotape. He was mortified. While you do not want to repeat his errors or create your own fiasco de jour, movement is a good idea. Use your feet to insure that you connect with the entire audience. Make confident movements— stage movement that accompanies a good eye scan of the room is always a good technique.

LANGUAGE

Every communication textbook that devotes pages to delivery addresses the need for skill in language use. The need for skillful use of language is just as important in debate. In truth, the need for skillful use of language may be exacerbated by the time constraints faced by the participant in parliamentary debate. Words, after all, are integral tools for construction of your argument.

Be Clear

Clarity cannot be underestimated. Imagine the speaker using ambiguous terms! What a boon for the opponent! This is especially critical when defining terms in the debate. Both the pro- and con sides of the debate question have to articulate precise and clear meanings of terms in order to properly build the most convincing case.

Be Concise

One of the challenges of parliamentary debate is leaving verbal pauses behind. The breaker words interrupt our sentences and arguments. For example, uhs, ums, like, whatever, right, ok, and so can fill up a great deal of time that could be used to enhance your argument. Additionally, these breakers or nonfluencies may make the speaker appear less able than others and reduce one's credibility.

Be Colorful

Framing your arguments by choosing colorful terms helps shape the perceptions of the audience and judges. By colorful, I do not mean profane but descriptive. The more vivid and directive the phrase, the better the steering of the perception of the judge will be. The speaker needs to be active and assertive in tone and word choice. This raises your credibility with the audience and judges. However, do use good judgment. Continual use of powerful language causes deafness by overload. Emphasize the terms that need to be emphasized, not those of lesser consequence.

HUMOR

James Thurber was reputed to have said, "Humor is a serious thing. I like to think of it as one of our greatest earliest natural resources, which must be preserved at all cost." The sentiment closely reflects the ties of humor and parliamentary debate. Humor in parliamentary debate is a skill to be practiced, best when researched, and wickedest in its most acerbic form, heckling. Humor is one of parliamentary debate's greatest assets and perhaps one of the most distinguishing characteristics of this debate format.

One example of humor in debate occurred on the campus of Valdosta State University (VSU). The VSU Debate Team hosted the British team in 1998. Although the VSU students were well prepared, spoke eloquently, and presented numerous facts and figures to build their case, they had one missing element, humor. The British debaters used quick wit and incorporated numerous references in their speeches and points of information to gain attention from the audience while supporting their point simultaneously. At the conclusion of the debate, the Brits won, largely due to their use of humor, confidence, and aggressive style in the competition. Humor will carry you a long way in a debate when used effectively and appropriately.

In this section, we look at when to use humor, when to heckle, and what type of humor to use.

When to Use Humor

One of the public assets of parliamentary debate is its ability to entertain in addition to inform. It could be said that the very nature of the activity lends itself to that entertainment component. We all have felt the endorphin rush from a good laugh or even a healthy chuckle. The key is to know when to amuse and when to avoid humor. You may notice that the word *amuse* is used in the previous sentence. It would be an error in judgment to seek belly laughs with each use of humor. Chuckles can be just as effective.

One of the most obvious opportunities to use humor is with points of order or points of information. Even a request can be phrased in a humorous way. It is a time for quick wit and quick thinking. For example, a debater might suggest in a point of order that, "Do you really believe that President Bush is concerned about every coral reef in the world?" However, do not allow your quit wit to move into blatant ad hominem insults, homophobic references, or other forms of discriminatory jokes or slurs. While these may get laughs, these jokes will serve you poorly with your judge and often your public. In some cases, these comments may be so damaging that the judge will cast the ballot for the other team and tarnish your reputation with the community.

It is appropriate to use humor early in your speech and at the conclusion of your speech. This tells the audience and judge that you are prepared, bright, and worth consideration. Many speakers have forgotten that humor on a topic may be researched just as evidence may be researched. The printed sources and web sources for humorous material defy counting. The key is to develop a repertory of stories, brief examples, and quotations that can apply to a range of topics. While memorization may be for many a lost art, it can be a special aid for you. Being well read and quick to apply that knowledge in a humorous way will set you apart from others.

When to Heckle

Heckling in parliamentary debate usually refers to the interruption of the speaker with a skillful barb or action. The first key in knowing when to heckle may be based in tournament rules or regional norms. Some tournament locations are much less receptive to heckling. If the tournament uses community judges who are not prepared for heckling, the response could be extremely negative. If manners seem paramount, then use heckling sparingly. If the atmosphere is more open, always monitor the reaction of the judges and audience. Too much heckling or repetition will become annoying and work against you. Most judges did not just crawl from under a rock! For example, the common cry of "shame" will become a sham if exercised too often.

Other verbal insertions need to be well timed and relevant to the argument expressed. For instance, "shame" and "here-here" should not be overused. These expressions should be timed for the pivotal places in the debate when key points are brought up by your opponent. Remember that heckling is not always about disagreement. It is equally appropriate to support the argument made by your partner through slapping the table or desk, stomping of the foot, or rapping of the knuckles. The use of shame, here-here, and tapping on the desk seems to be on the wane. There has been a recent push in the activity, especially in the Western U.S. regions, to focus more on substance and content in the debate over traditional stylistic features that were once closely observed.

On a cautionary note, do not heckle your partner or present an adversarial role to your partner. While it may be tempting to use humor, even biting humor, you will be ill served by even subtle jibes at your partner. Over the last few years in parliamentary debate rounds, I have judged a few teams where a more experienced debater lampooned his or her partner in one of the rebuttal speeches with comments similar to "Let me comment on point A since my partner is blind" or "In a rookie mistake . . ." Sometimes these are more humorous than stinging, but I take a dim view of such obvious jibes. It will not gain you speaker points.

What Type of Humor to Use

Stories, brief examples, quotations, and some single words can all be effective tools for humor. These need to be generally relevant to the subject or activity. Stories need to be short due to time constraints but can still be effective. These usually present some parody, irony, or unusual circumstance. Avoid puns and blatant insults. Puns are by nature moaners and usually only amuse the punster. Ad hominem insults alienate the opponent, perhaps the judge, and certainly parts of the audience.

Humor well used is an asset to the activity as is good language and delivery skills. Parliamentary debate is a wonderful activity that allows you to grow your skills in these areas. With practice, research, and wit, you can improve your debating career.

References

Leathers, D., & Eaves, M. H. (2008). *Successful nonverbal communication: Principles and Applications*. Fourth Edition. Boston, MA: Allyn and Bacon.

Chapter 3

Fallacies and Reasoning

Key Terms

AD HOMINEM
AD POPULUM
AD VERECUNDIUM
APPEAL TO FORCE
CANNED CASES
FALLACY OF ASSUMPTION
FALLACY OF EQUIVOCATION
FALLACY OF TRADITION
FALLACY OF THE
    RED HERRING

FALSE CAUSE
FALSE DICHOTOMY
HASTY GENERALIZATION
INDUCTION
METAPHOR
NON SEQUITUR
STRAIGHT RESOLUTION
TAUTOLOGY
WEAK ANALOGY

After examining the refinement of delivery in Chapter 2, we now turn our attention to ways to improve your reasoning skills in the debate. In addition, there are several fallacies that you need to be able to recognize in your opponent's speech. The following are several of the more common fallacies that are typically found in the debate. See if you recognize any of the following in this chapter, try to avoid using these fallacies during your speech, and point out fallacies that your opponent commits in his or her debate.

COMMON FALLACIES IN DEBATE

- **Ad Hominem**—the debater attacks the opponent's person, rather than the content of the argument. For example, you might say that you think their argument is stupid or "Southerners are stupid." In both of these examples, you personalize the debate. One form of ad hominem is "needling" or an appeal to one's personal charm. For example, in the 2008 Vice-Presidential Palin–Biden debate, Sarah Palin was seen winking to her audience. This nonverbal gesture was her way of making an appeal to personal charm.

- **Ad Populum**—the debater makes an appeal to the majority of society who support an argument. For example, if you were advocating environmental policy change, you might say that the Gallup poll shows that 67% of the U.S. public reject President Obama's policy on the stimulus package. Further, you might innocently say, "All my friends say that . . ."

© Yuri Arcurs under license from Shutterstock, Inc.

Avoid personal attacks of your opponent in the debate.

- **Ad Verecundium**—the debater places special emphasis on the source used for the claim, arguing that the validity of the claim is assured by the expertness of the source. In other words, you might argue in a debate that the study should be considered valid solely because of where the study took place (e.g., on Harvard University's campus).

- **Appeal to Force**—the debater argues that something bad will happen to you if you reject the argument. For example, you might use a fear appeal to convince the judge that a depression is imminent or you must reject patriarchy at all costs or that it is a moral imperative that we act now as policy agents.

- **Appeal to False Authority**—This fallacy is the opposite of the ad verecundium fallacy mentioned earlier. A popular fallacy committed in parliamentary debates, this fallacy uses vague references to the source of the claim or argument. For example, a debater might say, "I read this somewhere," "I heard this on the news," or "scientists believe that . . . " None of these appeals to authority can be easily discounted because the reference is either false or too vague to rebut. Many debaters now reference names of scholars or at least the source of the authority to avoid committing this fallacy in the speech.

- **Argument by Question**—This fallacy occurs when a speaker asks a question that does not have a quick answer. You can make your opponent look weak or ill prepared by this fallacious reasoning. This is a popular form of fallacy used during the point of information. A speaker can also ask a loaded question. For example, "has the government ever stopped bailing out the citizens?" The fallacy here is that the government bails out its citizens.

- **Cliché Thinking**—A derivation of the ad populum fallacy, cliché thinking is when the debater makes an appeal using a proverb or wise saying. For instance, when a speaker says "a bird in the hand is worth two in the bush" or "birds of a feather flock together," a cliché has been formed in the debate as fallacious reasoning.

- **Fallacy of Assumption**—the debater makes a faulty assumption in logic. For example, you might think that the Government's case goes through the federal government, but in fact the plan works through the United Nations. Here, you commit a faulty assumption that hurts your credibility and could possibly lose the argument at hand.

- **Fallacy of Equivocation**—the debater is inconsistent on his or her stance in the plan, claim, or case. For example, if the prime minister states in the constructive speech that the plan costs no money and then argues in the rebuttal speech that some money will be necessary to fund the plan, the debater has committed the fallacy of equivocation.

- **Fallacy of the General Rule**—If something is generally true, then it applies in every possible case. For instance, the statement that all chairs have four legs is generally true but not in every case. A bar stool with three legs or a rocking chair with no legs are both cases in point.

- **Fallacy of the Red Herring**—the debater diverts attention from the issue and draws a new conclusion based on that diversion. For example, you might say that the economy does not matter but the benefits are more important, thus the judge should reject economic reasons in favor of the benefits of the plan.

- **Fallacy of Tradition**—the debater makes an appeal to tradition. In other words, you might argue that a policy is good because it has always been done in this state, but not give supporting evidence of the benefits or advantages of the proposal.

- **False Cause**—the debater wrongly labels the cause of the problem. In other words, instead of labeling the cause of environmental pollution as the failure of industry standards, they label the problem as community neglect.

- **False Dichotomy**—the debater makes a faulty juxtaposition between a pair of words in the debate. For example, the debater creates a dichotomy between freedom and laws, instead of freedom and life.

- **Hasty Generalization**—the debater makes an inferential leap in logic from one chain to the next chain in the reasoning process. For example, you might argue that the Government case should be rejected because the plan causes a recession that leads to a nuclear war. The chain between recession and a nuclear war is clearly a hasty leap in logic.

- **Non Sequitur**—the debater's argument does not follow to the next logical point. For instance, you might say the Government wants to provide incentives for customers to buy certain products and then you say that the products are being banned in Mexico.

- **Reductive Fallacy (oversimplification)**—This fallacy usually happens when the debater does not clearly articulate the links in the argument. Traditionally, this fallacy might have been referenced as an argument without a warrant. For example, if someone says that "bailouts are robbery," this is a form of oversimplifying the government's current role in providing financial assistance to lenders, automakers, and other institutions.

- **Scapegoating**—the debater argues that a third party is to blame for the problem. For example, you might try to pin the problem down on liberal policy makers instead of facing the true origin of the problem.

- **Slippery Slope Fallacy**—the debater sets up an argument wherein future occurrences would always meet the standard and would infinitely entrap a number of unwanted or unintended consequences. For instance, if national security should be a paramount concern over individual privacy, this would set up a slippery slope: privacy would always lose out in the future, eroding one of our most precious individual rights.

- **Tautology**—the debater mindlessly repeats the same concept or is excessively redundant in his or her speech. For example, if the debater continues to state that the economy is improving, later says that the economy is better, and last says that the economy is looking good, he or she has in essence said the same thing three times, using different words.

- **Weak Analogy**—often used in parliamentary debate, since the debater depends on untraditional forms of evidence in this style of debate. For instance, you might say that the plan is beneficial and will help the economy grow in the same way that fertilizer helps grass grow.

Now that we have a good idea of the various fallacies used in debate, let us examine the types of reasoning that can be incorporated in debate.

REASONING IN PARLIAMENTARY DEBATE

Most of the reasoning that occurs in parliamentary debate today is **induction,** or reasoning by example. Most debaters will take a topic and find examples to prove or support the more general topic. Regardless of whether your topic is a **straight resolution,** a topic with directional focus, or a **metaphor,** a topic with little if any direction, you will want to use induction to help support your resolution in the debate. Since induction is reasoning by example, the parliamentary debater will want to find examples to support the topic. Let's look at how the topic reasoning might occur for the two principal types of resolutions.

First, there is inductive reasoning for straight resolutions. This is the type of resolution where most if not all of the direction to the topic is provided in the wording of the resolution itself. For example, let's say that you drew the following resolution for your round: This House Believes That President Bush Needs to Rethink His Strategy in Iraq. In this resolution, the Government and

Opposition teams both know the direction of the topic. The Government team knows that they will have to address policy change in Iraq from the executive level. The Opposition team has several options: they can either defend the current Bush policy or suggest an alternative to the Government proposal in the form of a counterproposal or counterplan.

Second, there is inductive reasoning for metaphoric resolutions. This type of resolution, although losing popularity in regions of the country, provides little if any direction to the topic. When parliamentary debate began in the early 1990s, these topics were the only ones used at tournaments. The problem became that there was not fair division of ground, and Opposition teams were left in the dark wondering what the debate would be about, thus muting any preparation time that they were afforded before the round began. At the same time, however, it should be pointed out that there are regional differences about using these types of resolutions. Some coaches and tournament directors have defended the use of metaphors on pedagogical grounds, arguing that it requires debaters to think on their feet and reduces the likelihood of research saturation or prepped arguments being brought into the house chambers.

When using metaphoric resolutions, the Government team has to first interpret the resolution and "spin" the topic into a debatable, controversial subject matter. For example, if the debate resolution for the round is "This House Would Ban It," the Government team would have to interpret the topic and decide what item they would want to ban or eliminate. One idea might be to lift the tariffs on imported goods. Yet another example of a metaphoric resolution might be even more vague. For example, what if the Government team drew a topic, "This House Believes That a Bird in the Hand Is Worth Two in the Bush." Here, the resolution is so vague that the Opposition would have no idea what the debate would be about. The Government team would have to interpret the topic to support the statement. Often times, when Government teams are given vague resolutions they will default to what are called **canned cases.** Canned cases, although not referred to in that way in the debate, are prepared and planned arguments that have often been used more than once in other debates and perhaps have been tested with some degree of success. Canned cases are often viewed as controversial and since many in the parliamentary debate community see their use as educationally destructive, these same critics have advocated the use of straight resolutions instead of metaphoric resolutions to avoid this dispute.

Chapter 4

Research

Key Term

ARGUMENT BRIEF

Research has always been an important part of academic debate. However, as discussed in Chapter 1, some in the activity felt that the evidence replaced debaters' arguments. Parliamentary debate sought to place a larger emphasis on the arguments made by debaters. That does not mean that there is no place for research in the activity. This chapter examines the importance of research, how to gather and organize research, and how to present research in parliamentary debate.

IMPORTANCE OF RESEARCH

Knowledge is power. In a battle of wits and words, the more you know about a topic the better. Parliamentary debate, like most things on a college or university campus, is primarily an educational activity. It is one of a few activities that link education to competition.

A competitive educational activity requires the participant to meet certain ethical standards. Most campuses have policies that prohibit plagiarism and other forms of academic dishonesty. While participating in debate, members of the campus community have the responsibility of following those standards.

In addition to campus standards, the debate community also has certain other standards. As in any community, the debate community has many different people and personalities. Within that community, you might be held responsible for your behavior. Lying and other forms of academic dishonesty will follow you. Dishonest arguments do not just hurt an individual debater but they could also hurt the reputation of your partner as well. Debate partners have a responsibility to be ethical out of respect for their partner (Swift, 2008). It will either hurt your self-worth or lead to a bad reputation in the community.

In addition to a bad personal reputation, presenting misinformation can lead to other bad outcomes. Arguing from assertions is the same as lying. Presenting information that is inaccurate does not educate the audience. Misinformation can lead to things such as stereotyping. However, engaging in the creation of sound honest argumentation helps the competitor learn to practice good ethical standards (Swift, 2008).

Within the community, you will find that many individuals are happy to share information with you. Teams often share theory arguments and knowledge with each other. The best way to be shut out of this educational setting is to be perceived as an unethical debater.

With ethics in mind, it is essential for debaters to have access to information about a variety of issues. In parliamentary debate, debaters are allowed to present "... any information that is within the realm of knowledge of liberally educated and informed citizens" (NPDA Rules, 2008). Some in the past have discouraged research arguing that arguments are more important than knowing specific information. However, the community has moved beyond this way of thinking. Arguments should be based on sound information possessed by the debater. The only type of knowledge not allowed to be presented in the round is personal knowledge, which not all the debaters have access to (NPDA Rules, 2008).

Beyond the personal satisfaction of knowing that you present information accurately, there are other advantages to good research. Topics in parliamentary debate change during every round. Issue knowledge is important for developing sound arguments for and against a variety of propositions. Nothing is worse than being defeated in a debate because your opponent simply knew more than you about a subject. However, the reverse is a great feeling. The hard work you put in is important for winning debate rounds.

Gaining knowledge on an issue is not enough. You must read information on both sides of the issue to help develop arguments. Debate often attracts students who have strong opinions about politics. Whether they are liberal or conservative, debaters often find themselves arguing a position that is antithetical to their personal beliefs. Within a debate round, you must be comfortable presenting both sides of a controversy. When students are outside of the debate community, they can use their holistic understanding of issues to make better arguments for their side. Understanding the arguments your opponents are likely to make allows you to prepare for them and counter them before they are even made.

The practice of debating and researching issues also proves an individual's critical thinking skills. Garside (1996, p. 215) lists four types of aspects of thinking that make it critical:

(a)   thinking that is clear, precise, accurate, relevant, logical, and consistent

(b)   thinking that reflects a controlled sense of skepticism or disbelief of any assertion, claim, or conclusion until sufficient evidence and reasoning are provided to conclusively support it

(c)   thinking that takes stock of existing information and identifies holes and weaknesses, thereby certifying what we know or don't know

(d)   thinking that is free from bias, prejudice, and one-sidedness of thought

Shutterstock © Utemov Alexey. Under license from Shutterstock, Inc.

The debater needs to read much material to be informed.

Allen, Bekowitz, Hunt, and Louden (1999) reviewed several studies about critical thinking and participation in speech and debate. Participation in debate enhances a student's ability to think critically. Enhanced critical speaking skills will help you in debate rounds and in everyday life. You will be able to better evaluate political, media, advertising, and other arguments. These skills are important for your participation as a citizen in any democratic government.

GATHERING RESEARCH

The wide variety of issues discussed in parliamentary debate requires a number of different research approaches. This section discusses approaches for gathering research on current events, political issues, and philosophy.

Current events research is a fairly simple process. Many students simply read a newspaper every day. Others have the team generate lists of current event topics and have individuals do in-depth research on each topic. It is best to do both to have an extended knowledge of current events.

When choosing a newspaper to read, it is important to choose a paper that has strong national, international, political, and editorial sections. Often debaters read more than one newspaper to accomplish these goals. Some American newspapers such as the *New York Times* and the *Washington Post* are popular choices because they cover a broad variety of issues. Sometimes debaters choose to read other newspapers to gain a greater understanding of international issues. Popular papers with strong coverage of international news include the *Christian Science Monitor*, the *Jerusalem Post*, and the *Times* (London). In addition to papers, students often read weekly news magazines.

For more specific research on issues, you can follow headlines daily. Websites such as news.google.com and news.yahoo.com show headlines and also allow you to search a variety of news sites for more in-depth research. Other services offered by your library such as LexisNexis allow you to search several newspapers at one time as well.

When doing newspaper-based research, the debater should understand that some articles simply repeat the same information as others. For example, many newspapers draw information from wire services such as the Associated Press (AP), Reuters, United Press International (UPI), and Xinhua (China). Stories written using wire services share similar information. In addition, papers owned by the same company, such as the Times Syndicate, often share national and international stories.

When reading stories, it is important to keep track of statistics and other information that can help you develop arguments. Beyond developing your own arguments from articles, it can be extremely helpful to read arguments made by others. You can start by making sure you read editorial articles while reading the paper daily.

Other good sources for arguments and information include books, journals, and think tanks. When a current event issue is recurrent, such as North Korean nuclear testing, books can often be valuable resources. While the information in books is often over a year out of date, books provide invaluable background information. Authors often make arguments about the success or failure of decisions made to deal with problems.

Journals, like books, are not as current as newspaper articles. However, they can provide much more in-depth information. For example, *Foreign Affairs* contains detailed articles on contemporary international issues. Authors are usually experts in the area. The journal format allows for longer articles so that they can discuss issues at length.

Think tanks, like journals, offer experts in their field the opportunity to discuss issues at length. Think tanks usually employ researchers who believe in a certain political ideology. For example, the Heritage Foundation, a noted conservative think tank, offers several articles and publications that support their side on a variety of issues. Think tanks also offer some nontraditional viewpoints. The Cato Institute is a libertarian think tank that focuses on constitutional issues. Think tanks are useful for finding authors who make specific arguments that you can use to bolster your own arguments.

Sometimes, no matter how much reading you have done on an issue you will still know little about a topic. Most tournaments allow you to use the Internet during preparation time. Encyclopedic websites such as the CIA World Fact Book and wikis provide quick general information on topics. Looking at a wiki is the last resort. The Internet and electronic media resources constantly change. Keep up to date on where news is posted. Reading about issues is the best way to keep oneself informed and ready to debate.

Beyond current event research, debaters often find that value or philosophical arguments are useful. A discussion of the types of arguments often made in debate rounds can be found in Chapters 6 and 7. Every discipline has a number of theories and philosophies. Communication scholars have based their arguments on theories from prominent philosophers in their own discipline such as Michel Foucault. Do not abandon the knowledge you gain from your own educational experience.

SORTING AND ORGANIZING EVIDENCE

New debaters often find organizing and accessing their research much more difficult than obtaining the information. There are several ways to organize the massive amount of information that you gather. One way to organize your information is a traditional paper file. Paper files are often discouraged because they require a lot of paper and ink, filing is time consuming, and files are difficult to transport. However, many teams compete in both debate and individual events. Extemporaneous speakers often keep a paper file so that both debaters and extemporaneous speakers can work out of the same files.

A paper file requires competitors to print out their research. Research is then organized into file folders. File folders are often divided into boxes of international and domestic issues. Files are usually placed in alphabetical order.

Debaters can also use computer application or simple file folders to keep track of their research. There are several applications available for organizing research. Whether students use a database system or simply save articles into file folders, electronic files are easily transferred from one computer to another. They are also more portable than electronic files.

Debaters cannot read everything. However, reading information is the best way to keep oneself informed. When there is too much information for one person to read on key issues, teams often write outlines, commonly known as briefs or talking points, to summarize information. Briefs should include important facts, statistics, and historical points about the issue. For each piece of information, you should write down the author, the author's credentials, the source, and the date.

In addition to fact-based briefs, competitors often develop argument briefs. As noted previously, different styles of arguments including affirmative cases and disadvantages are covered in Chapters 6 and 7. Argument briefs are used to minimize the amount of preparation time spent on developing arguments before the round so that debaters can discuss how to strategically use the arguments during the debate round. The practice of writing positions ahead of time is often called canning positions. In the parliamentary debate community, the practice of canning is not always viewed as acceptable. Yet some tournaments encourage preparation beforehand. For instance, the fall tournament at the University of Wyoming announces their topic areas a couple weeks before competition begins.

USING EVIDENCE

Since parliamentary debate in the United States set out to differentiate itself from evidence-based debate, the use of evidence during preparation time and during the round has always been a controversial issue. There is no standardized practice for accessing evidence before the round. Most tournaments will allow debaters to access any resource, including people, during preparation time. However, some tournaments do not allow coaching during preparation time.

Shutterstock © Konstantin Chagin. Under license from Shutterstock, Inc.

The team works here to find evidence on the computer during preparation time.

During preparation time, managing your time is essential. Since it is illegal to bring actual evidence into the round, it is essential to write down all arguments and evidence you plan to use in the round. In addition to materials listed in the previous section, it is important to have access to a dictionary and a copy of the United States Constitution. You cannot read evidence word for word; you must paraphrase it in your own words. The paper you write your arguments on is the only thing you can reference during the round. You cannot bring anything to the round except arguments written by you and your partner and a copy of the NPDA Rules (2008).

During preparation time, it is also important to make sure that you understand the position you put together and how the evidence fits with it. Often, beginning debaters read the outline they write down word for word or repeat what their coach tells them word for word. It is easy for an opponent to show this weakness during the round.

Despite the fact that there is no rule against citing evidence during the presentation, some regions of the country discourage it. Ask your coach and critic before the round how they want you to present evidence. When you cite evidence, some teams will argue that you are presenting information outside the realm of common knowledge. That is why it is important to keep a copy of the NPDA Rules (2008) with you. Specifically, rule 4 describes how to use evidence during the debate.

When discussing a common event such as when a Supreme Court decision was made or when a war started, you need not cite sources. However, when citing statistics and opinions you may find it necessary to cite your sources. At a minimum, you need to cite the name of the source and the date.

When presenting quantitative research, case studies, arguments from editorial, and philosophical arguments, there are five simple steps that allow you to present research accurately. First, incorporate the statistics, facts, argument, and/or philosophy into the presentation. Second, state the name of the author, the source, and the author's qualifications (i.e., medical doctor, research fellow, etc.). Third, mention the date of the article you obtained the information from. Fourth, mention and explain the research and how it fits with your arguments. Do not just restate exactly what the author said. Finally, balance the research and your arguments designed specifically for the proposition being debated.

SUMMARY

While there are no set standards for presenting research, research is still an important part of parliamentary debate. You have an ethical and educational responsibility to present accurate information in the round to support your arguments. Research is time consuming but is an important part of debate. Each region of the country has different opinions about how evidence should be presented in the round. Make sure that you adapt to your critic so that you can effectively present research in the manner he or she expects you to. Finally, use evidence to support your arguments and not to argue for you.

REFERENCES

Allen, M., Berkowitz, S., Hunt, S., & Louden, A. (1999, January). A meta-analysis of the impact of forensics and communication education on critical thinking. *Communication Education*, *48*(1), 18. Retrieved June 1, 2009, from Communication & Mass Media Complete database.

Garside, C. (1996, July). Look who's talking: A comparison of lecture and group discussion teaching strategies. *Communication Education*, *45*(3), 212. Retrieved June 3, 2009, from Communication & Mass Media Complete database.

NPDA Rules of Debating. (). (2008)Retrieved August 29, 2009, from http://www.parlidebate.org/npda-rules/

Swift, C. (Summer 2008). Theory, application, and pragmatism: ethical issues for Directors of Forensics and National Parliamentary Debate (NPDA). *Forensic*, *93*(2), 39–59. Retrieved June 3, 2009, from Communication & Mass Media Complete database.

Chapter 5

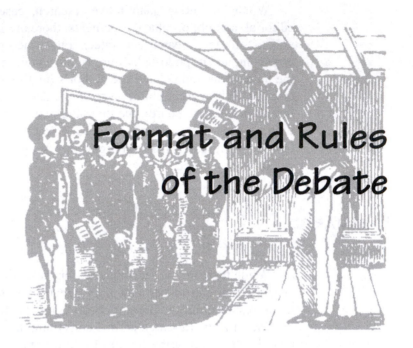

Format and Rules of the Debate

Key Terms

Proposition
Opposition
Prime Minister
Leader of the
    Opposition
constructive
rebuttal
prep time
topics
defining
squirrels

praxis
clash
opposition block
point of clarification
points of order
points of personal privilege
points of information
point not taken
point taken under consideration
point well taken

There are many styles of parliamentary debate across the globe. The structure and style followed here are that of competition of styles in the United States. In parliamentary debate, two teams each made up of two competitors represent two sides, the Proposition and the Opposition. The task of the Proposition, formerly known as the Government, composed of the Prime Minister and the Member of the Proposition, is to uphold the resolution, whereas the task of the Opposition, composed of the Leader of the Opposition and the Member of the Opposition, is to deny the resolution. Each team supports its own arguments and proves false the arguments of the other.

Each round consists of prep time, constructive speeches, and rebuttal speeches. In addition to these, participants may raise points of order, points of information, and points of personal privilege. The Prime Minister of the Proposition and the Leader of the Opposition have two speaking opportunities, one constructive and one rebuttal, while the Member of the Proposition and the Member of the Opposition each have one constructive speech. All members of the debate may raise the points mentioned above. Each round is timed, generally lasts one hour, and follows this structure.

Speaker/Event	Speech type	Length (min)
Prep time		15–20
Prime Minister	Constructive	7
Leader of the Opposition	Constructive	8
Member of the Proposition	Constructive	8
Member of the Opposition	Constructive	8
Leader of the Opposition	Rebuttal	4
Prime Minister	Rebuttal	5

No preparation time is available between speakers in parliamentary debate. Now let us examine each of these elements individually followed by the points of order, points of personal privilege, and points of information.

PREP TIME

The first order of business in any round is the resolution. Sample topics may be found on various web sites, including those listed on Debate Central at the University of Vermont and the past resolutions link on the NPDA web site. In some competitions, only one resolution is given for the participants in the round and must be debated, whereas in others, three topics are offered and each team is allowed a strike. The third topic is then the one debated. After topic selection, each team must read the resolution. This starts the creative act of debate. The amount of prep time varies by tournament, with fifteen minutes at some locations and twenty minutes at others.

Although each team must define the key words of the resolution (it helps to have a pocket dictionary), the teams decide the parameters of the resolution. The Proposition must decide according to the resolution the definitions of the key terms and their interpretation, what they are to prove, what they are *not* to prove, and what the goal of their argument will be. This goal is sometimes called a case statement.

In contrast, the Opposition must, while still defining key terms and discussing the resolution, focus on the construction of the resolution. What does the resolution mandate the Proposition accomplish, regardless of their case construction? This should lead to a discussion of the burdens of proof for the Proposition. Additionally, the Opposition should consider any philosophical or applied opposition to the praxis of action or understanding proposed by the resolution. Finally, the possibility of squirrel interpretations (or extremely creative interpretations of the resolutions) requires the Opposition to prepare to present another alternative to the Proposition's case.

Depending on the tournament and its association, the teams may or may not be allowed published information in the debate chamber during the round. In addition, this may include prepared case documents and general reference materials such as dictionaries. For all constructive speeches in the debate, the first and last minute of the speech are protected from interjections from the opponent in the debate. These inquiries are known as points of information. While points of order and points of personal privilege can be raised in the constructive speeches, their occurrence is rare.

PRIME MINISTER (SEVEN-MINUTE CONSTRUCTIVE)

The responsibility of the Prime Minister during the first seven minutes is to set the parameters for the Proposition case or to define the motion and to present the case of the Proposition. The Prime Minister normally opens with acknowledgements of the Speaker of the House (Madam or Mister!), the Opposition, the Speaker's partner, and members of the audience (Parliament). The Prime Minister then moves to the full constructive.

It is critical to remember the skills attached to public speaking here. In contrast with other forms of debate, speed is not a necessity, nor even desired–nor is the alienation of the Opposition or audience through inappropriate sarcasm. The best introductions of the constructive draw from the tested methods found in countless speech texts, some form of attention getter that ties to the definitions and the case presented by the Proposition. Then, depending on the strategy taken by the Proposition, the Prime Minister may begin with definitions of key terms (especially if those are integral to understanding the outline for the case and the case itself) or with the outline of the case with the definitions to follow.

Finally, it is the burden of the Prime Minister to provide areas for clash. Failure by the Prime Minister to set up a constructive speech providing opportunity for clash defeats the purpose of parliamentary debate; arguing. Without clash, there is no debate.

LEADER OF THE OPPOSITION (EIGHT-MINUTE CONSTRUCTIVE)

After the Prime Minister finishes, the Leader of the Opposition rises to give the first speech of the Opposition. After starting with greetings such as those of the Prime Minister, the Leader may agree or disagree with the motion as presented by the Prime Minister, including the definitions of key terms. The essential elements of the Leader's constructive are the presentation of the Opposition's view and the deflation of the Proposition's case. In either of these, clash should become apparent. The philosophy of the Opposition should obviously differ from that of the Proposition. The deflating of the Proposition's case should be accomplished through attacking the premises and evidence presented in the Prime Minister's constructive speech. While the Opposition may provide through its philosophy or view an independent case, it does not have to do so. All that may be required to win the round are successful attacks against the Proposition. The Opposition attack with a solid independent view is often referred to as an "offensive" maneuver. Relying solely on attacks against the case are usually called a "defensive" move. More and more, parliamentary judges prefer the Opposition team to have an offensive strategy over the more feeble position of solely attacking the proposition's case.

Finally, it is equally the burden of the Leader of the Opposition to provide clash in the round. While the Prime Minister must provide areas for clash, the Leader must create the dispute with the Proposition position. Again, without clash there is no debate.

MEMBER OF THE PROPOSITION (EIGHT-MINUTE CONSTRUCTIVE)

The Member of Proposition is not required to greet the members and participants, as are previous speakers. The central tasks of the Member are to uphold the Proposition's case, to counter the objections of the Opposition, and to add additional lines of reasoning supporting the Proposition's case. Throughout these tasks, the Member of the Proposition should also attack the view and evidence of the Opposition.

The Member should be especially concerned with extending the case for the Proposition rather than falling into the trap of restating the Prime Minister's case. This would be particularly critical if the Leader of the Opposition has nullified the Prime Minister's case. In addition, the Member must emphasize the critical points in the debate that will be important in the Prime Minister's rebuttal.

MEMBER OF THE OPPOSITION (EIGHT-MINUTE CONSTRUCTIVE)

This final constructive is in some ways the most challenging of the four constructive speeches. The Member of the Opposition must react to all three of the previous speakers. The direction of the speech is determined both by the success of the Leader of the Opposition in destroying the Prime Minister's case and by the success of the Member of Proposition in expanding or defending the Proposition's case. The Member of the Opposition must at least continue to address the objections raised by the Leader, but depending on the flow of the round, the Member may need to refute new arguments presented by the Member of the Proposition.

Of special concern to this speaker is the decision regarding the introduction of new ideas into the round. The Proposition in the Prime Minister's rebuttal may treat ideas introduced here. The decision to introduce new ideas should be considered carefully, for the Opposition will have no opportunity to speak out in answer to that rebuttal, for it ends the round. The final responsibility of the Member of the Opposition is the same as that of the Member of the Proposition, to emphasize the arguments to be presented by the Leader in the rebuttal.

LEADER OF THE OPPOSITION (FOUR-MINUTE REBUTTAL)

The primary purpose of the rebuttals is to assert the superiority of the positions of the side of the speakers. In the case of the Leader of the Opposition, we would emphasize the role of the Opposition's team on major issues and why these positions are superior. The Leader of Opposition rebuttalist should crystallize the debate and reduce the round to voting issues (or "voters") for the speaker of the house.

PRIME MINISTER (FIVE-MINUTE REBUTTAL)

If the Member of the Opposition has the most challenging constructive, then the Prime Minister has the greater challenge in rebuttal. Coming on the heels of twelve minutes of Opposition speaking time (often referred to as the *opposition block*), the Prime Minister's rebuttal must attempt to clinch the round for the Proposition. The ability to analyze the Opposition's arguments and strategy is critical here. The Prime Minister must selectively answer the Opposition's arguments or at least demonstrate the superiority of the Proposition's position on those central, selected points of clash.

These speeches should reflect the accepted forms of public speaking. Each should introduce the material therein, give the main points of argument and support, and emphasize the keys of the speech in a conclusion. Remember that the objective is to persuade the House (the judge).

Points of Order, Points of Personal Privilege, and Points of Information

One of the more interactive parts of parliamentary debating is the ability of the sides to interject into the speech of the opponent. Often an entertaining and strategic element of parliamentary debate, these interjections are known as points and include points of order, points of personal privilege, and points of information. Points of order and points of personal privilege are relatively rare, while points of information are common practice. Practice and strategy for using these distinctive elements should not be ignored.

Points of Order

A participant raises a point of order when an opponent has violated a rule of debate. These violations usually include complaints about speaking time and complaints about new arguments introduced during rebuttal. The clock is stopped so that the current participant is not deprived of time. Normally this point is not debatable and must be decided upon by the Speaker of the House immediately. This ruling may be in support of the point ("Point well taken"), against the point ("Point not well taken"), or indecisive ("Point taken under consideration").

While, by rule, the Speaker of the House or judge should rule immediately, local customs may vary. Some judges allow or even expect the point of order to be addressed by the participant charged with the violation. Some go even further and allow time for brief debate from both sides. After the arguments from both sides, the judge will issue the ruling. Other judges choose to question the participant raising the point in order to evaluate its merit and then issue a ruling. If a critic is uncertain as to the ruling, a default response might be to say, "I will rule on this at a later time in the debate." This ruling will allow the issue to be "fleshed out" in more detail without making an ill-prepared ruling that could affect the debate's outcome.

In responding to the point of order, the participant receiving the point should respond only based on the judges' decision. If the point is "not taken" or is "taken under consideration," then the participant may continue. However, if the point is "well taken," then the speaker must stop the offending behavior immediately. Therefore, if the violation is a time violation, the speaker must finish very quickly and sit down. If the violation is one of new argument, the speaker must move to another point of rebuttal.

Failure to challenge rules violations can make a debater appear either uninterested or uninformed. In either case, failure to raise appropriate points of order damages their recognition as a speaker in the balloting and in the awarding of speaker points. Further, failure to raise valid points of order may enable your opponent to pursue an inappropriate course of action to defeat you in the round. Remember, if you raise the point, your opponent must allow the interruption.

Conversely, raising spurious points of order will damage the debater raising those points. Raising points that may not have substance can appear to be a bullying tactic or a move of desperation. Raise points when you are confident of the violation.

Points of Personal Privilege

Points of personal privilege are raised if a participant believes that a competing speaker has seriously abused the argument or has insulted someone. This point is not debatable by the accused and must be ruled upon by the

Speaker of the House. Points of personal privilege are relatively rare, but they can serve to identify inappropriate behavior in the round.

For example, several years ago, we knew of a round where two former romantic partners were on opposite teams. While humor should be encouraged, crudity or loutish behavior should not. The comment in question during the round suggested, though indirectly, a lack of male sexual prowess. The opponent certainly had the right to raise the point of personal privilege though not by offering to demonstrate on the spot the falsity of the insult. Neither person behaved appropriately.

Responses by the judge are the same as those given to points of order. A judge may issue an immediate ruling or allow debate on the rules violation and then render the decision. In addition, the judge may question the person making the point, analyze the rules violation, and then make the decision.

In addition, reacting to the point of personal privilege is similar to points of order. If the point is "not taken" or is "taken under consideration," then the participant may again continue. If the point is "well taken," then the speaker must stop the offending behavior immediately.

Points of Information

Points of information are one of the more energizing elements of parliamentary debate. Points of information may ask for clarification (sometimes referred to as a point of clarification) from the person speaking or may give a comeback to the idea expressed by the person speaking. The participant wishing to make a point of information stands facing the person speaking, with either a hand out or verbally calling for a point of information. The person speaking may take the point of information (allowing the question or statement) or refuse to take the point, continuing the speech. If the speaker refuses to take the point of information, the participant must sit down. Points of information are not allowed during the first and last minute of the constructive speech and are not allowed during rebuttals. Signaling behavior as designated by the judge will signify the first minute and last minute of the constructive speeches in which the points of information may be raised. The judge most often slaps his or her hand on the desk to signify the point of information period is open or closed.

When a speaker accepts an opponent's call for a point of information, the speaker must remember that the clock continues to run against the speaking time. The reason for this is that the speaker is not required to yield the floor. The opponent's point should be brief and to the point. The speaker may answer the point or ignore the point based on his or her judgment regarding the success of the round.

Refusal to accept points of information, although the prerogative of the person speaking, may be seen as defensive behavior. Failure to offer points of information may also make the participants seem disinterested in the topic or debate. The best course of action: be involved and engaged in the debate, especially in the competition.

A lingering question for many debaters is whether to phrase points of information as questions or as statements. Both are correct forms, but the statement provides you the opportunity to make the argument needed. Either form may be a useful vehicle for humor. The humor used in these points needs to show your wit, not a penchant for crudity. In addition, you may need to discuss the issue with the judge before the beginning of the round. The parameters of acceptance are likely to differ with each judge from those unwilling to have heckling to those who encourage the use.

Points of information may also be used strategically. If your opponents cannot be understood, a point of information is in order. After all, how can one argue against unclear arguments or reasoning of a case? Furthermore, points of information can serve to identify errors of fact in your opponent's speech or even points on which the opponent agrees with you. Certainly, a point of information phrased to demonstrate that the opponent is making your point could be crushing to their side.

Responding to points of information strategically is equally important. An opponent may raise the point of information to distract you and lead you away from your argument. If you choose to answer, be brief and direct. If you choose not to answer, be equally clear, without equivocation, which empowers your opponent for constant interruptions. Put more simply: say "no" or "not at this time," to cite a popular convention to respond to an overly energetic or inopportune question during your speech. Take points of information at a time that fits your speech design. You may pause briefly to provide an opening for the question.

Furthermore, remember that points of information provide the speaker with valuable opportunities. You may indeed need to clarify your argument or information. You may be able to demonstrate the paucity of understanding or knowledge of your opponent. You may be able to respond with a sharper wit than that demonstrated by your opponent. Points of information make parliamentary debate lively.

Chapter 6

The Proposition Case

Key Terms

advantages

attitudinal inherency

criterion

counter criterion

directional-focus resolution

existential inherency

fact cases

inherency

metaphoric resolution

policy cases

plan

significance

solvency

straight resolutions

structural inherency

truism

value cases

Now that we have discussed the format and rules of debate, let us turn our attention to the construction of the Proposition case. This chapter will be divided into two main sections: 1) topic interpretation and 2) types of cases. Responses and pre-emptions to typical Opposition claims will be discussed at the end of the next chapter on the Opposition's case.

TOPIC INTERPRETATION

Perhaps one of the most important variables to the success of a Proposition team in debate is the interpretation of the topic or resolution. In most parliamentary debates there are three types of resolutions: straight resolutions, directional-focus resolutions, and metaphoric resolutions. **Straight resolutions** are topics that provide precise and clear policy action for the debate round. Often times, these resolutions are so precise that they rely on the debaters' knowledge of laws or recent news accounts to be able to effectively debate the topic. The national trend as of the writing of this book is for the increasing use of straight resolutions at tournament.

What do straight resolutions look like? A straight resolution that might be used in a debate is, "This House Believes That the United States Federal Proposition Should Lift Trade Restrictions on Steel Imports." This example provides a clear agent of action, the Proposition, and also suggests what the action of the agent is to be: lift trade restrictions on steel imports. Another example of a straight resolution would be, "This House Believes That the United Nations Should Expand the Amount of Building Contractors to Help Reconstruct Iraq." Similarly, this resolution provides a clear agent and action for the Proposition team to undertake in the debate.

A second type of resolution, and one of the most commonly used nationwide, is the directional-focus resolution. A **directional-focus resolution** is a topic that provides some degree of direction for the debate, but not enouth to overly limit the topic interpretation. One example of a directional-focus resolution is, "This House Would Change the Court Decision." In this topic, the Proposition team has to overturn a court decision, but is not told which decision. Thus, Proposition teams would have a considerable amount of ground to interpret which decision to overturn and decide the impact of making such a decision. Another example of this type of resolution might be, "This House Believes That the Emphasis Placed on Security Has Hurt Personal Privacy." In this topic, the Proposition team is given a clear direction for what side of the debate to defend, yet is afforded the leeway with which to decide what area of security has cost some element of privacy. This type of resolution is popular with most tournaments as it combines the freedom and thought of creativity with the restraint on bizarre and imaginative topic interpretations.

The final type of resolution is the metaphoric resolution. A **metaphoric resolution** is a topic that is broad and vague and provides a virtually limitless interpretation for the Proposition team. This type of resolution, due to the vagueness of the topic, is the least-used resolution in parliamentary debate because it unfairly hurts the Opposition's ground for knowing what the topic or direction of the topic might be during the preparation period before the debate begins. A few regions across the U.S. use metaphors more often than any other topic, but most regions are moving to directional-focus resolutions or straight resolutions.

A good example of the metaphoric resolution might be, "This House Would Be in Left Field." This topic places little if any restriction on the Proposition's interpretation of the topic. The only restriction on the discussion is that the resolution asks that the house be in left field. Since this statement is a metaphor, the Proposition team need only to explain how their focus is unusual or atypical, thus meeting the heart of the metaphor or cliché, "in left field." Another example of this type of resolution might be, "This House Believes That Cats Are Better than Dogs." Since this statement is in itself a nonsensical and virtually impossible topic to debate literally, the Proposition team would only have to argue that some idea or value was better than the alternative.

In each of the three above topic interpretations, it is essential that the Proposition team choose a topic that is current, up-to-date, and, most importantly, controversial. If there are not two sides to the topic interpretation offered by the Proposition team, the Opposition team can offer what is formally referred to as a truism. A **truism** is when the Proposition team's topic interpretation is so abusive and one-sided that there is no room for debate. For example, in one debate, a Proposition team may argue that food is essential for life. Since the Proposition team defined the resolution in such a way that the Opposition has no ground to debate, the case is said to be truistic. The Opposition team would be forced to argue that food is not essential for life, an oxymoron to say the least. Another example of a truistic case would be if the Proposition team decided to focus on a policy from its home state (e.g., changing the deer hunting laws for Montana). This would be an unfair interpretation of the topic since the Opposition would not have a ready account of specific laws from other states. If these instances occurred, the Opposition team could successfully offer a challenge, often made as a point of order, to the Proposition team's interpretation, saying that it was truistic and not debatable (the point of order on grounds of truism will be discussed in further detail in Chapter 10).

TYPES OF PROPOSITION CASES

There are three types of Proposition cases that can be constructed in the Prime Minister's opening speech: **fact cases, value cases,** and **policy cases.** Each case is developed by the Proposition team depending on the resolution and the flexibility of the topic wording.

Fact Cases

Fact propositions ask arguers to prove the statement true or negate it. They are commonly identified by the use of the word *is*. For example, Resolved: The United States is the last super power. Fact propositions must have two sides; otherwise, they would be true statements. Resolved: The United States is holding prisoners at Guantanamo is not debatable because it is a true statement. The most common use of fact propositions is in the criminal court system. Lawyers have to prove or disprove fact-based statements such as Mr. Jones is guilty of first-degree murder.

Fact cases are designed to prove the proposition more true than false. Often times, these resolutions are seen as abusive and Proposition teams often do not choose to run fact cases. When they do, proposition teams must effectively convince the critic that the fact is likely true. The Opposition's ground in a fact case debate is to argue that the fact did not occur or that the proposition team did not offer enough evidence to prove the fact true. How would this play out if the topic was worded, Resolve: This House Believes the Media has Mislead the Public. For example, a fact case that the Proposition could run might be that the media has misled the public about political candidates. The burden would be placed on the Proposition team to show that the media somehow misinformed or deceived the public about a politician and his or her belief or stance on a particular issue. This topic might also involve the media's infatuation with a politician's background or sordid past or falsity with regard to characterizations made about the candidate.

Fact propositions often result in debates that boil down to a war of evidence. Teams try to present as many facts as possible in support of the resolution and do not evaluate how the facts fit into the debate. That is why it is important for the proposition team to offer a criterion. A criterion is some kind of standard offered by the proposition team explaining how arguments should be evaluated in the debate. This weighing mechanism should provide a clear way for the judge and other audience members to evaluate the debate. Preponderance of evidence is a criterion taken from the legal community. Instead of counting the number of facts, the preponderance of evidence standard, ask the critic to weigh evidence based on its probable truth value.

The leader of the opposition can always offer a counter criterion and argue that there is a better way to interpret how the facts should be evaluated. Without offering a criterion, there is no way for the judge to rule in favor of the proposition team because there is no way to weigh the facts they present in support of proposition.

Value Cases

Value propositions ask arguers to show that an idea or philosophy ought to be valued above another. They are commonly identified by the use of value laden and/or philosophical terms. For example, This House believes that when in conflict the United States ought to value liberty above safety. In the resolution, the idea of liberty needs to be compared to the idea of safety. Only situations where one might be substituted for another should be discussed.

When developing a value case, there are a few important components. First, it is important to identify and define the value you are advocating. When looking at the philosophies of liberty and safety, it is important to give the audience a framework to evaluate them in. Offering a value such as human rights gives the audience a way to evaluate the arguments. The criterion offered for a value case should link directly to the value you advocate. A criterion for this debate could be "which side, the proposition or opposition, promotes the most rights."

In addition to the value and criterion, contentions must be offered to support why one philosophy should be preferred to another. In the example, a proposition might argue that in times of crisis, focusing on individual liberty protects more rights than focusing on safety. Value cases are difficult because you must argue for a philosophical idea and what the potential outcome of using the philosophy might be. A successful value case always shows why one philosophy should be valued over another. An unsuccessful approach is a case that advocates only good things about their philosophy. Comparison is the key to proving the proposition true. Opposition arguments can show that counter philosophy meets the criterion better or simply argue that the proposition team has not proven that one philosophy is better than another.

Policy Cases

Policy propositions ask arguers to explain how a new course of action should be taken. They are commonly identified by the use of the words *should* or *would*. For example, Resolved: The United States should change its tax system. To prove the resolution true, a debater would have to show why replacing the tax system is needed. The debater would also have to show why a new tax system is better than the old one.

Perhaps one of the most popular and strategic approaches that Proposition teams can take, regardless of the type of proposition, . . . in parliamentary debate is the incorporation of the policy case. A policy case is a plan or proposal that is offered by the Proposition team in order to fix or help correct a problem in the current system. Policy cases are most often used when straight or directional-focus resolutions are used. Policy cases must include the following elements in order to meet requirements for most judges: significance, inherency, solvency, plan, and advantages or benefits.

Significance is the importance or impact of the problem that is stated. The Proposition team must be able to discuss how the stated issue impacts life or values and has consequences under the system. For example, if the resolution was, "This House Believes That the United States Federal Proposition Should Protect Its Coral Reefs," the Proposition team would have to establish significance in their policy case. Significance could be that coral reefs are key to the ecological systems and that without them we stand to not only lose an important natural resource, but also economic benefits such as tourism.

Whenever possible it is important to quantify and qualify your significance. Protecting coral reefs becomes even more important if the problem deals with several coral reefs. Also, the number of species that are impacted by the destruction of reefs is important. Be as specific with your information as possible.

Inherency exists when elements built into the system prevent the plan from being adopted now. This is one of those elements in the policy case that often times debaters take for granted but can be a key voting issue for some judges (this issue and various judging paradigms for evaluating inherency will be discussed in greater detail in Chapter 11).

There are three types of inherency: structural, attitudinal, and existential. **Structural inherency,** arguably the strongest form of inherency, is when there are institutional structures or laws that exist in the current system that prevent the plan from being enacted right now. For example, if the topic was, "This House Would Legalize Marijuana for Medical Use," the Proposition team might argue that the structural inherency is current laws set up in most U.S. states that forbid the use, manufacture, and distribution of marijuana for any reason.

Attitudinal inherency, the next strongest type, suggests that public opinion or polls indicate your policy case does not enjoy popular support. In other words, your attitudinal inherency for this case would be that the U.S. surveys show that the public does not favor marijuana legalization for medical use.

The final form of inherency, and the weakest type, is existential inherency. **Existential inherency** is when the policy or plan that the Proposition team advocates simply does not exist. Again using our example above, the existential inherency for this case would be that, currently, not all fifty states in the U.S. enjoy legalized marijuana for medical use.

The third essential ingredient to a policy case is solvency. This element is perhaps one of the most important issues in the construction of the policy case. **Solvency** means the workability of the plan. The Proposition team needs to show through use of examples and reasons that the policy advocated is workable and has the potential to be successful. In some cases, the Proposition may want to elaborate on solvency claims by referring to published sources or authors of special importance. The caveat here is that the Proposition team will have to be careful to avoid charges of specific knowledge, or claims that the material is too specific to be debated (this controversial issue will be elaborated in Chapter 9).

The fourth ingredient to good policy case construction is the **plan**. Although fine, specific elements are not required, basic mandates and funding mechanisms may be necessary for the debate on a policy case. The specificity in the plan is decided case by case, and can always change with judge variations and demands. The plan should always be written out in a text form to reduce the chances of the Proposition team mutating the plan and becoming a moving target for the Opposition to attack.

While plans can be stated in a couple of sentences or in outline form, a typical plan includes the following elements. The agent in the plan is the actor who has the power to approve the course of action. Often when dealing with domestic issues, the United States Congress would be the agent. The second part of the plan is the mandate. The mandate is the part of the plan where exactly what action will be taken is explained. Mandates need to be as clear and specific as possible. Enforcement is the part of the plan where the proposition team explains who will make sure the plan actually happens. The enforcer is often different from the agent. For example, if the federal proposition lowered the speed limit on interstate highways, they would have to rely on state patrol

officers to enforce the policy. Finally, most plans need funding. Without a way to pay for the costs of a plan, it is unlikely that an audience would be persuaded to enact it.

The final element to a policy case is the discussion of benefits and **advantages** of the policy action. Advantages are the positive outcomes of the plan or policy action. It is important for the Proposition team in the Prime Minister's opening constructive speech to carefully articulate what the advantages and benefits are of the new idea or proposal. These ideas need to be carefully explained to persuade the judge to vote for you and to allow the judge to weigh the potential benefits of action with the potential harms or disadvantages of the policy (the disadvantages of policy action will be discussed in greater depth in Chapter 7).

FINAL THOUGHTS

In practice, debaters and judges often agree that the affirmative team has the right to define the debate. For example, Brodak and Taylor (2002) argue that fact resolutions should never be debated because of the impossibility of a debate round to determine the validity of a single fact. However, traditionally the idea of a trichotomy (fact, value, policy) of types of propositional statements has guided the practice of intercollegiate debate. In many situations if competitors can justify why they feel that a resolution should be presented as a fact, value, or policy resolution, they can argue it as such. The opposition team, of course, has a right to dispute that idea.

It is important to understand that not everyone writes an affirmative case exactly the same way. However, just like in any other discipline it is important to learn common terms used in debate. These explanations will help you build cases on a variety of topics. When debating, an opponent may not use the same outline or even terms. The most important thing for a competitor to do is to make arguments. When arguing yourself or listening to opponents, do not get hung up on the terminology; listen for the arguments that are made.

Finally, it is your responsibility to be clear. Remember the advice levied given in Chapter 2. If you cannot deliver your case clearly to the judge and opponents, you will not win the debate. Walton (2001) notes that "Debaters attempting to enhance their credibility with big words, baffling jargon, and run-on sentences undermine their central purpose. . . Debaters may well understand their case, but that alone does not translate into a useful discussion." Proposition teams that are not clear will likely lose the debate.

REFERENCES

Brodak, G. W., & Taylor, M. (2002). Resolutions of fact: a critique of traditional typology in parliamentary debate. *Journal of the National Parliamentary Debate Association*, 7. Retrieved June 8, 2009, from http://www.parlidebate.org/pdf/vol8no2.pdf

Walton, J. D. (2001, February). "Making the case" tips for affirmative case construction. *Rostum*, 75(6). Retrieved June 8, 2009, from http://debate.uvm.edu/NFL/rostrumlib/WaltonFeb%2701.pdf

Chapter 7

The Opposition's Case

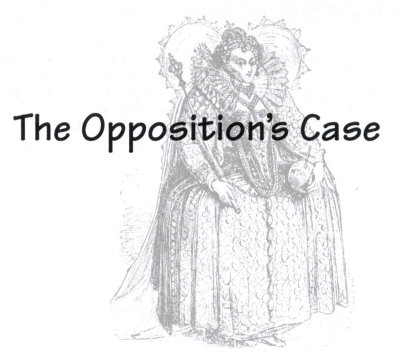

Key Terms

agent counterplans
critique
counterplan
delay counterplans
disadvantage
effects-topicality
extra-topicality
Government critiques
impact
language critiques
link

movement counterplans
mutual exclusivity
net beneficiality
non-topicality
permutation
plan-inclusive counterplans
social critiques
sub-topicality
topicality
uniqueness

Now that we have looked at how to build the Government case, let us turn our attention to the Opposition's case. The chapter is divided into five main sections and will cover in the following order, straight refutation, topicality (resolutionality), disadvantages, counterplans, and critiques. Following the Opposition's treatment within each section is the Proposition team's response to the issue.

STRAIGHT REFUTATION

One of the most traditional approaches to attacking the Government case is by straight refutation. **Straight refutation** is when the Opposition team goes directly down the arguments in the Government case one by one. The Leader of the Opposition leads the assault by defeating the Government's criterion, case contentions, and any advantages presented. Opposition teams begin with off-case arguments first, then go back to the Government case to attack its points one by one. Usually, this strategy is successful, but time consuming.

The most successful straight refutation attack is the turn-around or "turn" for short. When using this tactic, the Leader of the Opposition reverses the impact made by the case and literally "turns it around" in the face of the Proposition team. For example, if the Proposition team argued that ocean biodiversity is important because it assures life on earth, the Opposition could argue a turn-around by saying that protecting species hurts the environment since there is natural extinction in all planetary systems.

A less successful attack used in straight refutation might be to argue take-outs on case. In other words, the Government case may say that the economy is doing poorly now and the plan helps the economy. A case take-out would suggest that the plan will have no impact on the economy, thus taking out a potential advantage for the Proposition team. Overall, the turn-around is a stronger argument than the take-out since the Proposition team is forced to respond to the argument. Most importantly, if the Opposition team wins this argument, the turn becomes an independent reason to vote for the Opposition team in the debate.

TOPICALITY

One of the most hotly contested issues in debate is the topicality argument. Often times, in parliamentary circles, this issue is called the resolutionality argument or topicality. **Topicality** is an argument that suggests that

the Proposition team's interpretation of the debate falls outside the acceptable boundaries of the topic or resolution. This argument should be presented in the Leader of the Opposition's speech in order to be acceptable in the debate. Topicality can be elaborated upon in later speeches but Opposition teams should always present the issue early in the debate to provide ample room for discussion so that the argument can be fleshed out.

Within the topicality argument, there are four major types of topicality positions: non-topicality, extra-topicality, sub-topicality, and effects-topicality. **Non-topicality** is the most popular form of topicality and suggests that there is a word or phrase in the topic that the Proposition team violates. For example, if the resolution was, "This House Believes That the Government Should Reduce Environmental Emissions," the Opposition team might argue that the Government's definition of *reduce* was inappropriate or unacceptable for the debate.

Another form of topicality argument is extra-topicality. The **extra-topicality** argument is when the Opposition team states that the Proposition team is solving for some issue or concern beyond the realm of the topic. Using the same topic as above, the Opposition team might argue that the Proposition team not only reduces environmental emissions, but sets up new environmental policy that goes beyond the heart of the topic.

A third form of topicality is the sub-topicality. Probably the rarest form of topicality, **sub-topicality** is when the Opposition team states that the Proposition team is only solving part of the resolution's topic. If the resolution was that, "This House Should Advocate World Peace," and the Proposition team only assured peace in Europe, then the Opposition team could argue that the Proposition team was sub-topical since they only solved for peace in a part of the world.

The final form of topicality is the effects-topicality. **Effects-topicality** is when the Opposition team says that the plan itself is topical only through the effects of the action. If the resolution was "This House Should Protect Marine Resources," and the Government plan was to advocate iron fertilization for oceans, the Opposition team could argue effects-topicality. Since the plan (iron fertilization) does not directly protect marine resources, but only the "effects" of the plan protect other phytoplankton and aquatic life, the Opposition team could argue that the Proposition team's plan is topical only through the effects of action. The Opposition team should ask for the ballot due to the plan's topicality problem.

Government Responses to Topicality

There are many ways that the Proposition team can argue that the topicality argument is invalid. The most common ways are to 1) suggest that the plan meets the topic; 2) argue that the Opposition team's definition of a word is invalid; 3) propose a set of counter-standards on topicality; or 4) argue topicality is not a voting issue.

First, the Proposition team may strike down a topicality argument by simply suggesting that the plan falls within the limits imposed by the topic. By using a strategic definition of one or more of the words in the resolution, the Proposition team can successfully argue that the policy advocated, especially in the Prime Minister's opening speech, falls within the parameters of the topic.

Second, the Proposition team can suggest that the Opposition's definition of a word in the resolution is invalid. Of course, this assumes that the Opposition has stated an alternative definition. If a dictionary definition has not been offered by the Opposition team, the Proposition team can ask for the immediate rejection of the topicality argument. In the event that a definition was offered by the Opposition team, the Member of the Government will want to state in his or her speech that the alternative definition is invalid and suggest how the Government proposal meets the topic.

Third, the Proposition team may present a myriad of counter-standards that are often used to steer the critic away from linguistic concerns, toward more substantive issues in the debate. Such counter-standards might include showing that the Proposition team has a right to define and set up the debate in a reasonable fashion. In addition, the Proposition team may want to argue that they parameterize the resolution by stating the focus of the topic, thus nullifying any semantic disputes over terms or phrases in the topic. Lastly, the Proposition team could suggest that since the Opposition has fruitful debate elsewhere on the flow, that that is where the heart of the debate lies and a team should not be punished for a trivial difference between meanings of words.

Fourth, the Proposition team could argue that the topicality argument is not a voting issue. It should be noted that, as of the writing of this book, unlike policy debate, many parliamentary critics reject the topicality argument in the debate round. Thus, many Proposition teams can successfully argue that topicality should serve only as a guideline for the debate focus, not as a voting issue proposed by the Opposition team.

DISADVANTAGE

The next issue that deserves our attention is the use of the disadvantage in the debate round. Probably one of the strongest weapons that any Opposition team has, regardless of the topic, is the disadvantage. The **disadvantage** is a harm or problem that results from the Proposition team's action. For example, if the Proposition team were advocating a flat tax in the debate, the Opposition team might argue a disadvantage by saying that this policy is discriminatory since it favors the rich and hurts the poor. There are three essential elements in the construction of the disadvantage for the Opposition team: the link, the uniqueness, and the impact.

The **link** is the connection of the Government plan to the stated disadvantage. For example, if the topic says that "This House Should Reduce Global Warming," and the Proposition team decides to run an electric cars case, the Opposition team could argue that electric cars would hurt U.S.-OPEC ties since we would be reducing our dependence on foreign oil.

The **uniqueness** is when the Opposition team must show that we are currently not experiencing the disadvantage before the policy is passed.

In other words, the Opposition team here would show that current ties between the United States and OPEC are at record highs, thus indicating that the disadvantage is not happening now. This element of the disadvantage is often the weakest element in the argument and perhaps the one single element of the disadvantage that is the most taken for granted.

Finally, the **impact** is the seriousness of consequences that might result from the disadvantage occurring. If the Opposition team argues that the Government plan is too costly, what is the impact? A good Opposition team must be able to impact that argument by suggesting that costs will hurt businesses, lead to a recession, complicate budget deficit reduction, lead to a depression, or worse. The impact element of the disadvantage answers the question, "so what?"

Answers to the Disadvantage

The Proposition team has many options available when responding to the disadvantage argument. The most common responses to the disadvantage include a link take-out, a link turn, a non-uniqueness, an impact take-out, and an impact turn.

Initially, the Opposition team may offer a link take-out. A link take-out is when the Proposition team argues that the link connecting the Government policy with the disadvantages is absent or missing. This is a common strategy in responding to disadvantages but is a defensive position. A defensive position is a response that does not require a response in return by the other team.

Second, and a somewhat more aggressive strategy by the Proposition team, is to construct a link turn. Since a link turn basically suggests that the opposite results from the passage of policy, this is an offensive argument. An offensive argument is a response that demands a response by the Opposition team else it stands as an independent reason to vote for the Proposition team.

Next, there is the non-uniqueness argument. Here, the Proposition team merely suggests that the action or policy has been tried recently with no negative outcomes, thus nullifying the Opposition team's uniqueness of the disadvantage. For example, if the Opposition team says that the plan hurts freedom and liberty, the Proposition team could respond by saying, "Non-unique. There are currently lots of freedoms and liberties being reduced in the status quo with or without the Government plan." Like the link take out, the non-uniqueness is a defensive argument in the debate.

The Proposition team can offer an impact take-out position to counter the disadvantage. An impact take-out says that the impact or consequences of the policy are not likely or will not happen. For example, if the Opposition suggests that spending leads to a recession, which causes a depression, the Proposition team could argue an impact take-out by stating that recessions do not always cause a depression and that the connection to the consequences is fallacious. The impact take-out position is a defensive argument and can be dropped by the Opposition team without serious consequence.

Finally, perhaps one of the strongest Government responses to the entire disadvantage is the impact turn. The impact turn is when the Government "turns around" the consequences of the disadvantage and suggests that the opposite is true. For example, if the Opposition argues that the plan causes a depression, the Proposition team might grant that this is true, but then argue an impact turn by suggesting that depressions are good because they avert the chance of war. This position is an offensive argument for the Proposition team and cannot be dropped by the Opposition team.

COUNTERPLANS

Perhaps one of the most dynamic and versatile Opposition strategies in the debate is the use of a counterplan. A **counterplan** is a proposal or plan offered by the Opposition team to solve for the Government problem area. Typically, a counterplan has two burdens it must fulfill: non-topicality and competition.

First, most critics insist that counterplans be non-topical, else there are two topical actions presented in the debate and the critic would have no choice but to vote for the Proposition team. Some policy debate judges and coaches allow topical counterplans, but this condition only happens when the topic is bi-directional. For example, if the resolution was "The United States Federal Government Should Pass a New Penal System," the Proposition team could either increase or decrease a system whereby punishment is more or less severe. In some cases, the Government might do away with all penal systems. In parliamentary debate circles, resolutions are usually vague, abstract, and not bi-directional. Proposition teams are required to pick a topic area that is debatable, controversial, and timely.

Second, a sound counterplan must contain competition. A counterplan must compete with the Government plan or proposal. Competition occurs in two primary ways: mutual exclusivity and net beneficiality. **Mutual exclusivity** simply refers to the separation of the plan and the counterplan. If the two proposals cannot be separated, then they are not mutually exclusive. For example, if the Proposition team advocated United States action, the Opposition team might offer a United Nations counterplan. Since those actions could conceivably happen separately from one another, they are said to be mutually exclusive.

Net beneficiality is another requirement of competition. The Opposition's counterplan or proposal must solve for not only the Government's benefit, but an additional benefit as well (thus, the counterplan is net beneficial).

One popular way that Opposition teams run a net benefits standard is by using the standard of "avoiding the disadvantage." In other words, Opposition teams might run a disadvantage to the Government plan, alongside a counterplan. For example, the Opposition team might suggest that the Government plan causes a spending disadvantage, but the states counterplan offered by the Opposition avoids concerns over federal spending, thus the counterplan would be net beneficial.

Types of Counterplans

There are many types of counterplans, and each varies depending upon the Proposition team's interpretation of the topic and the wording of the plan. In general, there are four main counterplans: agent counterplans, movement counterplans, delay counterplans, and plan-inclusive counterplans.

First, there are **agent counterplans** or counterproposals that offer an alternative agent to that of the Government plan. For example, if the Proposition team offered a plan administered by the United States government, the Opposition team could propose an agent counterplan through the United Nations or NATO as alternative agents of change. Everything else in the plan would be the same, except for the agent used. These are popular counterplans since agent disadvantages are so common in debate.

Second, there are **movement counterplans.** Opposition teams might be helped by running a counter movement position in the form of a counterplan. Here, the Opposition offers a societal movement as an alternative to government action. Social movements, socialism, anarchy, and feminism are ways that the Opposition team could advocate a social movement position instead of government intervention.

Third, there are **delay counterplans,** which may be the most strategic yet controversial of all counterplans. Simply stated, the delay counterplan just enacts the plan at a later time. This counterplan works well in presidential or midterm election years. Often times, political capital or climate disadvantages are run during election years. The delay counterplan works in harmony with these disadvantage types since the counterplan would wait until after the election to avoid the political turmoil. It should be pointed out that many judges find little favor with these counterplans due to their abusive positioning in the debate.

Fourth, there are **plan-inclusive counterplans.** Equally controversial are the plan-inclusive counterplans. Like delay counterplans, plan-inclusive counterplans are moderately modified Government plans offered by the Opposition team. These counterplans include the rhetoric of the Government plan but take an additional step to solve the problem. This could be to change the funding or enforcement mechanism, or to add a small step in the mandates of policy action. These counterproposals are met with much Opposition and are rarely accepted in parliamentary debate circles.

Government Responses to Counterplans

There are many ways to respond to counterplans, but Proposition teams can generally rely on three primary strategies: 1) arguing that the counterplan is topical; 2) arguing that the counterplan does not compete; 3) arguing that the counterplan can be permuted with the Government plan; or 4) arguing that the counterplan has disadvantages.

One successful way to defeat a counterplan offered by the Opposition team is to argue that it is topical. If the Proposition team, usually in the Member of the Government's speech, can show that the counterplan action is topical, then there are two Proposition teams and the judge should vote for the Proposition team. In the case of a states counterplan, the Proposition team could argue that since the Proposition team uses all 50 states in their Proposition team plan, that the counterplan is at a minimum effectually topical and at most an out right topical action.

Another way to defeat a counterplan is to argue that the plan does not compete with Government action. Since competition is broken down into mutual exclusivity and net benefits, here the Proposition team could argue that the counterplan did not solve for any additional benefits, therefore should be rejected. The issue of arguing that the counterplan is not mutually exclusive is taken up in the next section on permutations.

A third way that the Proposition team can take out a counterplan is to permute the plan. A **permutation** is when the Proposition teams try to test counterplan competition by advocating the plan together with the counterplan. In other words, if the Opposition team advocated U.N. action against the U.S. action, a Proposition team could permute the U.N. action by stating that the U.S. could do the plan first, then do the U.N. action next. An additional way to permute the plan might be to do both at the same time. For example, the Proposition team could argue that since the U.S. is the primary holder in the U.N., it is impossible to separate these agents and therefore action is never mutually exclusive (therefore rejecting the counterplan by the Opposition team).

Last, the Proposition team can offer a host of disadvantages that are unique to the counterplan. Just as the Opposition structures disadvantages against the Government plan, the Government can offer disadvantages against the Opposition's policy in the debate. The Government has to be especially careful here not to construct a disadvantage against the counterplan that also applies to the Government plan. This is a common mistake made by Proposition teams who run disadvantages against the counterplan. For example, if the counterplan was state action, the Proposition team could suggest a disadvantage by saying that state action is corrupt and just makes the problem worse.

CRITIQUES

One of the newest and most popular forms of Opposition strategies in contemporary parliamentary debate is the critique. A **critique** is an Opposition argument that suggests that there is a fundamental flaw or framework that circumvents or stops the success of the Government action. In some instances, a critique is a "pre-resolutional" issue, although this is not always the case. A pre-resolutional issue implies that the Speaker of the House must first settle this dispute before moving to the substantive issues found in the case or plan debate.

In parliamentary debate, since the Speaker does not bring evidence to read, he or she has a lot riding on the credibility of linguistic choices and in-round demeanor. The student must carefully select the words to be used during the speech or in the point of information period. If a debater uses racist, sexist, or other offensive speech, he or she has damaged or lost any credibility attained to that point. Often times, this mistake can lead to a loss for that team. Typically, these examinations of language choices are called critiques. There are three main types of critiques in a debate: language critiques, social critiques, and Government critiques.

Language Critiques

In **language critiques,** the Opposition team argues that the Proposition team should be punished for using inappropriate or offensive rhetoric in the debate. Since evidence in parliamentary debate is not stated from quotations (as with its policy debate counterpart), but from the debater's extemporaneous pool of words, the offense is that much more punitive in nature.

Many critics have decided to "regulate" the words of the debate, much the same way censors on television regulate or censor inappropriate speech. Debate judges can use paradigms that encourage debaters to use nonoffensive speech or lose the debate ballot. Some judges have been known to award no (zero) speaker points in an effort to send a clear message to the community, other team, and coach of the debaters' school that in-round language choices are a serious issue and violations of that standard will result in heavy consequences on the ballot. Debaters must adapt to such parameters, and realize the importance of judge adaptation (judge adaptation and paradigms will be discussed later, in Chapter 10).

Social Critiques

A second type of critique is known as the **social critique,** in which the Opposition team offers a philosophical position that counters the framework offered by the Proposition team. For example, the Opposition team could suggest a postmodern or feminist framework as a social critique for evaluating the debate.

In the postmodern critique, the Opposition argues that modernist thinking is inherent within the structure of the Government case or plan and, therefore, should be rejected. The critique suggests that modernism is unfair, unequal, oppressive, and dangerous. The Opposition team needs to remember to impact a social critique and suggest a possible alternative framework for workability or problem solving.

In the feminist critique, the Opposition team says that the Proposition team either uses sexist speech or fosters a plan that is entrenched in patriarchal or sexist structures. Plans or cases that advocate using the military are susceptible to feminist critiques since the literature points to an inherent male bias in military decision making. Since the Government case is flawed because it rests on such sexist foundations, the Opposition team can argue that the Government case should be rejected. In both examples of the social critique, the Opposition must explain the linkage between the Government case or plan and the negative impacts that result from such thinking.

Government Critiques

The final form of critique is called the Government critique. A **Government critique** is an alternative framework proposed by the Opposition that challenges the Government mechanism that the Proposition team advocates. These critiques are probably the least popular in parliamentary debate, due to their complex and philosophical nature. Yet, some liberal critics and judges have allowed debaters to construct and present such arguments in the debate.

One example of a Government critique is anarchy. Often run as a counterplan, the anarchy critique challenges the basic assumptions behind Government action. Another example is socialism critique. Once again, this critique suggests an alternative framework for solution and defends a socialist vision for change. In both examples of the Government critique, the Opposition team tries to persuade the Speaker of the House to embrace the non-Governmental alternative as the best policy to solve the problem.

Answers to the Critique

There are two basic methods for answering the critique: straight refutation and turns. First, straight refutation is the most popular method to respond to the critique. Often conducted in the Member of the Government speech, the debater attacks the critique by arguing down the flow point by point. While this is often the most effective way of defeating the critique, it is also the most time consuming and lacks an offensive element to its argumentation framework.

Second, and perhaps a more effective method overall, is the turn tactic. Similar to the offensive approach of attacking disadvantages, discussed earlier in the chapter, the turn-around can be used here for similar results. Since the argument presented in the critique is turned back in the face of the Opposition, they must answer the argument, else the turn becomes an independent reason to vote for the Proposition team. This "offensive" element in the turn is what provides its strategy and unique approach in effectively responding to critique-type arguments in the debate.

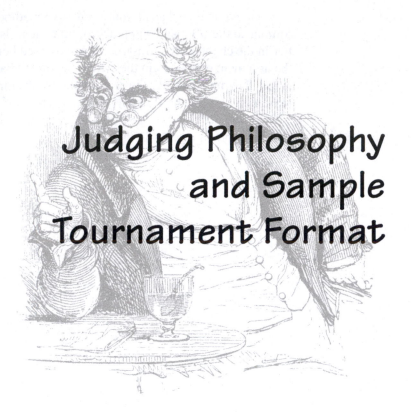

Chapter 8

Judging Philosophy and Sample Tournament Format

AUDIENCE ADAPTATION AND JUDGING PHILOSOPHY

Audience adaptation stands as one of the most central concerns of any persuasive endeavor. Whether in class, at home, or while on the job, one's ability to adapt to an audience is critical in moving the audience to adopt your plan or action. This is just as true in debate. However, the pivotal audience in almost every round is the judge. In some tournaments' audiences, especially in final rounds, a panel of critics must be persuaded, and usually the only audience of concern is the single judge.

Adapting to judges is largely a matter of understanding judging philosophies. For years in parliamentary debate, the use of vague and metaphoric topics seemed to limit judging philosophies since critics were reduced to merely weighing "who sounded the best" or "who did the better speaking." With the expansion of topics into straight and directional focus topics (as previously discussed in an earlier chapter), the judges are playing a significantly more important role in evaluating policy-type arguments in the debate. For instance, how one views topicality or evaluates the merits of a counterplan in a parliamentary debate varies tremendously from judge to judge. Thus, some parliamentary tournaments, especially at the national level, are starting to require judging philosophy statements and use preference sheets to allow debaters to "select" their ideal critic when so much is riding on a decision. A *preference sheet*, as often used in policy-debate circles, is a list of the judges who will be used in the tournament. Debaters and coaches for each school fill out a team or school wish list by ranking the judges A, B, or C according to their relative strengths and desires for the said critic in the debate. This process makes the judge's selection and clear philosophy statement that much more important, because this process usually requires written philosophies to be on file for participants to view before making their selections.

A judging paradigm is an assessment tool for debate. Judges may see debates as mock trials or a courtroom scene. Others see debates as competing ideological systems. Still others work from a type of cost-benefit analysis. This chapter reviews recognized judging philosophies and offers ideas for adapting to these philosophies. Remember that the skilled persuader adapts to the audience. Your audience is the judge, and adapting to their paradigm is essential to your success. Since not all tournaments use preference sheets when making their judging assignments, debaters must be able to adapt to a variety of judging styles in the community.

There are many judging paradigms and philosophies, but generally there are only five major types. They include The Scientist, The Philosopher, The Critic, The Amnesiac, The Gamer, and The Speech Teacher. Each of these paradigms is discussed in detail in the following sections.

The Scientist

The scientist or hypothesis tester focuses on the notion of true or false. The more specific question is whether the government's case is true or false based on the hypothetical extensions of the case. This posture is of course friendly to the opposition. The opposition has the task of showing any element of the government case false and in so doing wins the round. In some rounds, the opposition may even be able to question the provability of the case in order to win. This is due to the burden on the government. The government must prove its case is true because in the scientific approach, if a proposition in not proven true, then it is false. The presumption in the debate always rests with the opposition team under a hypothesis tester's paradigm.

One strategy for the Proposition team to adapt to this judge would be to set limits on testing the hypothesis that will prove their case. An example of this strategy would be to establish that any improvement in the environment would be in the public interest, thus the policy should be adopted. It would be difficult to argue successfully that we all need to move to bicycle transportation, but reduced emissions from limited driving could be argued to improve the environment. A second strategy, though riskier, is affirming that any change brought about by the case is sufficient. This is similar to the idea of the comparative advantage case (previously discussed in Chapter 6). A third strategy for influencing the scientific judge is to set strong value criteria in addition to affirming a plan. This is similar to the idea of the value criterion case (previously discussed in Chapter 6). If the round is close, the value statements might be enough to move ahead of the opposition.

Another example of hypothesis testing can be more proactive on the part of the debaters. In other words, some resolutions lend themselves to hypothesis testing. If for example a fact resolution were selected, the proposition team might want to argue that the resolution can be proven true, thus the case should be adopted. If the topic was Resolved: The New Deal was beneficial for America, the proposition team could provide an example(s) to justify that the hypothesis is true. On the other hand, the opposition team could provide examples where the New Deal failed, thus hoping to negate the hypothesis and proving the resolution untrue.

Overall, the opposition team has an easier burden to bear with this type of judge than does the proposition team. Opposition speakers first need to decide if the government has properly framed its case or if the opposition can attack the government on this point. If the opposition can show that the government has improperly framed its argument, then the judge will vote for the opposition. A second adaptation is for the opposition to show that the government is not treating all members of the population fairly. For example, if the government proposes to treat combat veterans for a certain malady, but not support personnel, then has the government prepared an adequate case?

Another strategy for the opposition is to argue that the government has made a hasty generalization. A hasty generalization is an argument whereby the debater suggests that the opponent has sidestepped a key linkage in the argumentation (this fallacy was discussed earlier in Chapter 3). With parliamentary customs prohibiting directly quoted material in the debate, this argument could be a potent weapon. Claiming insufficiency of example or evidence is difficult for the parliamentary debater on the government position to defend. In addition, the opposition may raise value objections or point out disadvantages in the government plan. If claims of falseness cannot be managed, then the opposition can still claim that societal values make the plan a bad choice among options.

The Philosopher

The philosopher or ethicist provides a second rubric for judging. Essentially, the philosopher decides the round based on philosophical grounds from the government and opposition. Presumption for this judge is on the side of the government, if the government sets justifiable criteria and then makes arguments to be on case inside those criteria. For this judge, the government does not have to defend the resolution as truth, but it has to be consistent with the resolution.

The government can adapt to this type of judge by showing the greatest impacts resulting from their arguments. If then, the government can show that more good comes from their plan than can be shown that bad will come, the judge goes to the government for the round. A second adaptation is to insure that the government produces strong criteria for judging the case. It then becomes the burden of the opposition to offer superior criteria or accept the criteria of the government, a result that often ends with the judge supporting the government.

The opposition can adapt to this type of judge by arguing impacts. This notion of impact is not limited to severity or large amounts of damage or the idea of something bad. It may include the notion of no effect. If the case has no impact, then the government may be accused of squandering resources.

The Critic

The critic focuses on the quality of the argument without the trappings of a philosophical system or the notion of the hypothesis tester's truth. The quality of the argument is not based on the topic. Instead, it is based on the quality of the debater's analysis of the topic, along with the quality of examples and the arguments on impacts. Adaptations for all competitors should be framed by the judge's reactions.

This paradigm would embrace a balance between looking at the strength of the argument and the delivery of those arguments. Since analysis of topics and evaluation of impacts involve delivery and speaker skills, this judge would rely heavily on critiquing the debaters' use of gestures, vocal skills, and overall persuasive tactics employed throughout the debate. Since the points of information and order are vital to any parliamentary debate, the Critic judge would evaluate those questions and answers to those inquiries more closely than the average judge.

The Amnesiac

Tabula rasa or "blank slate" judges approach debate as though they are completely open with minimized preferences. This goal of openness allows the judge to follow the argument made by debaters to address the issue as a self-contained knowledge base. In essence, this judge pretends to know nothing in order to be taught and persuaded by the superior team. The adaptation for both sides for this judge is to pay careful attention to definitions of terms and of the topic, statements of value, and impacts. The debater gets to persuade the judge regarding what is good or bad. Once the government establishes the definitions of terms and topic, in addition to its plan, the burden on the opposition is to refute the government. If the opposition cannot refute those arguments, the government wins, regardless of how absurd its position may be. An adaptation for the opposition is to argue regarding the terms of the debate. If the opposition successfully argues that the judge has learned nothing appropriate to the topic (argument is not about topic) from the government, then the opposition wins.

This can be a voting issue for the tabula rasa judge, but not in all cases. This critic, unlike other judges, can view topicality as either a voting issue for the opposition or see a definition of terms to be merely a position that topicality should serve as merely a guideline to the discussion with no voting issue ramifications.

The Gamer

Another type of judge is one who regards debate as a game or contest. The overarching standard is that of fairness. The debaters must agree on the rules of the debate in order to "play." The round then goes to the debaters able to argue best under the rules. However, if a team has or takes an unfair advantage of this paradigm, the judge may vote against that team for not playing fairly.

One example of a Gamer in debate would be that fairness be the overarching principle that guides the decision process. In other words, the debaters (not the critic) must decide and agree to the rules of the debate. These rules can change from round to round, since fairness is vague and can be controversial from team to team. As long as the debaters make arguments that create an opportunity for either side to win, the Game theorist is happy. Whether that includes the debaters not using catch-22 dilemmas to win points, that topicality is not seen as absolute but as a debatable point that either side can win, or that disadvantages or counterplans can be supported by government or opposition team argumentation, the Gamer will be satisfied.

The Speech Teacher

The Speech Teacher places emphasis on communication skills in addition to arguments. These judges have a very heavy public skills orientation and evaluate heavily on whether the arguments made can be managed by the general public. All speakers should be ready to adapt to this judge by thinking through the complexity of the argument, the basic skills of speaking, and the type of language used in public discussion.

Since parliamentary debate has an unwritten rule that speech rate will be slow and conversational, the Speech Teacher paradigm is popular in this type of debate. Debaters will want to use appropriate lexicon that is not too advanced and adapts to a "lay audience." This adaptation is similar to the arguments and topics discussed in the "common knowledge" arena (as discussed in the last chapter). Speakers will also want to employ good vocal skills, appropriate gestures, strong eye contact, and a degree of professionalism when asking and answering parliamentary points that are raised throughout the debate.

FINAL TIPS

Adapting to the audience of most import, the judge, is one of the most intellectually stimulating elements in parliamentary debate. So how does one get ready to adapt? First, many tournaments require judges to submit judging philosophies to be published at the tournament. Studying these statements should help you generally organize your thoughts before speaking to that judge. Another tack is researching on the web. A simple web search produces a wealth of philosophies. A third option is tracking the points awarded by the judge at tournaments. It follows that speakers successful in those rounds meet the philosophy of that judge. What is it they did? Finally, and easily important, is the reading of the nonverbal behavior of the judge. Some judges disclose more than others disclose; however, be assured that if the judge looks bored, he or she probably is bored.

SAMPLE TOURNAMENT FORMAT

Competitive Debate
Many debaters travel to competitions that offer parliamentary opponents. There are regional and national tournaments. Those with smaller budgets and members on their team are more likely to attend regional competition, while larger programs attend both regional and national meets.

This chapter provides useful tools for parliamentary debaters and coaches who travel and participate in intercollegiate competition, regardless of program size. The chapter contains the following elements: (1) a sample tournament calendar for small and large programs, (2) a sample research and preparation schedule for squads readying themselves for tournaments, and (3) a sample tournament schedule for a school hosting an event on its campus.

Sample Tournament Calendar (Small Program)

Fall:

September—regional meet
October—state meet
November—regional meet

Spring:

January—regional meet
February—state meet
March—regional meet

Sample Tournament Calendar (Large Program)

Fall:

September—national meet
September—regional meet
October—national meet
October—regional meet
November—national meet
November—state meet

Spring:

January—national meet
January—regional meet
February—national meet
February—state meet
March—national meet
March—national meet
March—national championship

SAMPLE RESEARCH AND PREPARATION SCHEDULE

Each coach is different in how his or her squad researches and prepares for competition. The intensity of the preparation may vary depending on several variables including a national competition, unique area of unfamiliarity with critics, state meets, and national championships.

Typically, the week before leaving for the tournament is intense, and time and preparation are of the essence. We discuss a rough schedule that coaches may wish to adopt as a general guideline for tournament preparation and research. Each squad and coach is different, and the size and the competitive level of the tournament may dictate a more or less intense schedule. We include the week of the tournament from Sunday until leaving for the tournament on Friday.

Sunday

The coach may make an assignment for research briefs. Typically, the parliamentary squad will cover the major current events in economics, politics, medicine, legal, sports, or other main genres of news. The coach might review with the squad which teams are likely to attend the tournament, the judges or styles of the various judges who will be critics, and the styles and strategies of debaters and coaches who will attend.

Monday

The coach will want to have at least one practice round early in the week; we recommend by Monday. This way, the coach can identify potential problems with argument style, variation in delivery techniques, and methods of judge adaptation that might want to be employed for a successful competition at the tournament.

After the practice round(s), the coach may want to make another research assignment, which could be due just before leaving for the meet. After the practice round has concluded, the coach may discover a lack of familiarity with a given topic and will want to explain the issue further with the students and refine the style of argumentation or delivery to better adapt to the judges at the tournament.

Tuesday

The research briefs in the preparation file should be reviewed and up-dated. If there are old or new stories that need to be updated, Tuesday is a good day to be sure the evidence is in order. If the team wishes to run a new can case or polish a critique, the team needs to get these concerns out of the way early in the week.

Wednesday

By mid-week, all research briefs will be finished and reviewed with the team. Any gaps in the research need to be filled by the end of the day. The coach or professor will want to schedule another practice round and offer more in-depth criticism and recommendations for final polishing of delivery and argument techniques. This practice is especially crucial on Wednesday if the team plans to leave on Thursday for the tournament.

Thursday

On the final day of preparation before the tournament, the squad should tie up any loose ends in their preparation. The evidence file needs to be organized and reviewed for debaters' familiarity with the system upon arrival at the tournament. The coach or debate instructor may choose not to have a practice round this day (unless there was no practice round on Wednesday). The program director will want to review the proposition team and opposition team strategies with the squad members in a one- to two-hour session. A question–answer session could be integrated within this time to help students become more familiar with the information and better confident about addressing questions that may arise on points of information or order at the tournament. If there are any problems with the team's understanding of the case and off-case strategies, these concerns must be ironed out by the end of Thursday. Students could be asked to provide final research updates on Thursday, especially on economic or political news that changes routinely.

Friday—Day of Departure for the Tournament

Make sure that the students know and respect your departure time for the tournament. In addition, this rule holds true for on-campus debates and practices. By showing up on time, the director communicates the necessity of all students to adhere to departure times announced. While each coach has a different tolerance level for waiting on the day of the tournament, time is of the essence (especially if this is in the early morning hours). If repeated violations occur, the student should be reprimanded and possibly sanctioned from future travel with the debate class or team.

The professor should establish a travel policy and a squad handbook to address rules and regulations for student travel and behavior. This handbook should address guidelines for the team, how to prepare briefs and evidence, team demeanor at tournaments, and respect for authorities. The coach and director should insist on respect from students, and those who are disruptive either on or off campus should be put on probation or asked not to participate with the team. The goal of the debate team is to provide an educational arena for the students, not to fuel individual egos or personalities. The mission of your debate club or team should always be the coach's highest priority when values conflict with student agendas.

The following is a sample tournament calendar. We have used something similar to this calendar when hosting college events on our campus.

SAMPLE TOURNAMENT CALENDAR (HOST SCHOOL—THURSDAY TO SUNDAY TOURNAMENT)

Thursday

7:00–10:00 pm	early registration (tournament hotel)

Friday

12:00–3:00 pm	late registration (campus)
3:00–3:10 pm	general assembly
3:10–	announce topic for round one
3:30–4:30 pm	round one
4:40–	announce topic for round two
5:00–6:00 pm	round two
6:00–7:00 pm	dinner break
7:00–	announce topic for round three
7:20–8:20 pm	round three

Saturday

8:00–8:40 am	breakfast—coffee and donuts
8:40–	announce topic for round four
9:00–10:00	round four
10:00–	break
10:40–	announce topic for round five
11:00–12:00 pm	round five
12:00–1:00 pm	lunch break
1:00–	announce topic for round six
1:20–2:20 pm	round six
2:30–3:40 pm	break
3:40–4:00 pm	announce topic for octo-final round
4:00–5:00 pm	octo-final round

Sunday

8:00–8:40 am	breakfast (coffee and donuts)
8:40–9:00 am	announce topic for quarterfinal round
9:00–10:00 am	quarterfinal round

Sunday (continued)

10:00–10:40 am	break
10:40–11:00 am	announce topic for semifinal round
11:00–12:00 pm	semifinal round
12:00–1:00 pm	lunch break
1:10–	announce final round topic
1:30–2:30 pm	final round
3:00–??	Awards Ceremony (nice auditorium space)

SUMMARY

In this chapter, we examined the various judging philosophies of critics in the debate and how debaters need to adapt to the various styles. In addition, students should be familiar with how practice and debates evolve from on campus to intercollegiate competition off campus. The student and professor should always keep the mission of the club or group in mind when traveling and should always defer to the coach upon decisions made about travel, debate strategies, and debate team demeanor.

Exercise Section

C h a p t e r 1

Exercises

1. Discuss in class the importance of parliamentary debate's history. Do you see the NPDA as rebellious, or innovative? Why or why not?

2. What challenges would you like to see in intercollegiate debate? How can NPDA and its rich history work to serve that end and serve as a forum for that change?

Chapter 2

Exercises

1. Practice impromptu speeches with a group of classmates. Reserve a classroom and video equipment in order to tape your speech. Review and critique your delivery.

2. Compile a list of favorite humor websites. Test each for a range of topics that will allow you to develop your list of stories, examples, and quotations.

3.   With instructor or coach permission, practice heckling during one of their lectures.

| Chapter 3 | **Exercises** |

1. Look at a recent issue of your local paper. Read one of the stories on the front page. See how many fallacies you can identify from the chapter. How would you reword the claims or arguments to overcome these fallacies? Share this with the class.

2. Watch one of the talk shows on television that has a point versus counterpoint debate. Your professor may wish to provide more direction on this exercise as to the show or type of show you should watch. Next, decide which side commits the most fallacies in their presentation. Try to list these fallacies as you hear them on the show.

3. If you need to use poll data to support your speech or debate, how can you avoid the ad populum fallacy? *Can* you avoid the charge of an ad populum fallacy? How would you answer that criticism?

Chapter 4

Exercises

1. Do a research brief on a current topic in business, politics, or government. Be sure to include the pros and cons in your brief and any evidence citations that can be checked for accuracy and qualification.

2. Pretend you are on the Opposition team and the resolution you have drawn for the debate is This House Would Ban Marijuana Laws. Organize and structure an approach you might take on the Opposition side. Research the con side of this topic and report back to your class what your findings are.

3. Pretend you are on the Proposition team and the resolution you have drawn for the debate is This House Would Flee from Evil. First, try to interpret the resolution in a strategic way that is controversial and debatable. Next, outline an approach using a current event that meets the requirements of your resolution interpretation.

4. Have a practice round with your judge reacting to cause an adjustment to your balance between research and analysis. Discuss the round with the class.

Chapter 5

Exercises

1. Join with four classmates and decide on a current topic for research. After reading for an hour, draw for roles for a practice debate. Allow the classmate chosen to serve as Speaker of the House to define the resolution for debate. Conduct a practice round with reduced prep time and delivery time. Switch roles and debate again. In this practice round make sure you introduce points of order, points of information, and points of personal privilege.

2. Research a topic of interest. After your preparation, write a list of resolutions from the topic. Then practice framing arguments for each speaking role, by writing outlines for each speech.

3. Design a practice round in pairs of classmates for a topic that encourages points of information. Try to find at least five opportunities to interject.

4. Visit the humor websites you compiled in Chapter 2. Compose a list of appropriate expressions on a range of topics for use in heckling.

Chapter 6

Exercises

1. Using the topic, "This House Believes That the United States Should Send a Manned Space Flight to Mars," write a policy case. Be sure to outline the necessary elements of good policy case writing. Discuss your idea with the class.

2. Outside of class, watch a segment of C-SPAN or another government channel. See if you can decide what policy the speakers are advocating. Can you identify the inherency of the policy? Is there more than one type of inherency in the plan? Discuss this with the class.

3. Using the topic, "This House Would Shake a Tail Feather," create an acceptable Government interpretation of the topic. Outline the basic contentions of the case and how you would meet the interpretation of the topic.

4. Using the value resolution, "This House Prefers Freedom to Life," create a criterion and counter criterion that might be used by the debate teams. Which criterion does a better job of addressing the value claims in the resolution? Why? Explain the answer in small groups in the class. Elect a representative to state your reasons in front of the class. Discuss this as a class.

Chapter 7

Exercises

1. Using the resolution, "This House Supports Government Welfare," take an Opposition strategy in defeating that topic. Defend your strategy in front of the class.

2. What are the different types of topicality? Which types of topicality are the strongest? Form a topicality argument from the resolutional example in exercise 1 above.

3. Explain the difference between a counterplan and a critique. Come up with an example of each using the resolution above. Which approach is strongest? Why?

4. Why is it essential that the Opposition team run a disadvantage in the debate? What happens if there is no disadvantage at the end of the debate?

5. How effective are "turns" in debate? Why are they considered such an effective, offensive approach to responding to the Opponent's line of attack?

Chapter 8

Exercises

1. Compile a binder of judging philosophies from those found on the Web. Make a chart summarizing the common characteristics of the types of judges from the chapter.

2. Based on the philosophies compiled from the Web, compose your own judging philosophy.

3. With four others, stage practice rounds with a judging philosophy drawn by chance a few minutes before the round. Take turns serving as a judge, regardless of philosophy.

4. After participating in your first debate, do a judge-analysis of your critic. This might include summarizing key positions taken by your class judge or student critics. Try to develop an overall scheme for those balloted comments and see if you can decide which judging paradigm was used in the evaluation of your debate.

5. Which judging paradigm is the strongest evaluation method for your speaking style? Why or why not? Discuss your style with the class. How can you adopt your style to meet the demands of your least favorite paradigm?

Glossary

Ad hominem—a logical fallacy using a persuasive strategy attacking an opponent's character rather than answering the argument

Ad populum—a logical fallacy using a persuasive strategy claiming that if many believe a proposition, it must be true

Ad verecundium—a logical fallacy using a persuasive strategy focusing on the source of the claim or testimony

Advantages—the positive consequences of change advocated including its side effects

Agent counterplans—opposition proposes to act on the Proposition's plan with a different agent

APDA—American Parliamentary Debate Association

Appeal to false authority—fallacy using vague reference to the source of the claim or argument

Appeal to force—a logical fallacy using the specter of harm

Argument brief—a case outline

Argument by question—question used to create false impression of opponent by using an inquiry that is a double bind or is unanswerable

Articulation—saying a word distinctly and clearly

Attitudinal inherency—the argument that attitudes cause the problem or prevent the advantages rather than structures

Can case—prepared arguments for use at tournaments

CEDA—Cross Examination Debate Association

Clash—point of dispute in debate

Cliché thinking—fallacy of making an appeal using a proverb or wise saying

Common knowledge—general knowledge of a topic gained by reading public sources

Comparative advantage case strategy—when the proposition team proposes action that adds benefits to the status quo, with fewer negative consequences

Constructive—any of the first four speeches designed to build arguments

Cost-benefit analysis case strategy—argument demonstrating that benefits outweigh costs or that the costs are greater than the good obtained

Counterplan—solution offered by the Opposition when it agrees with the problem presented by the Proposition

Counter criteria—alternative standards offered to evaluate the truth of a claim

Criteria—standards used to evaluate the truth of a claim

Critique—technique of questioning values and the actions to which those values lead

Debate—a formal contest often in an educational setting in which the affirmative and negative sides of a proposition are advocated by opposing speakers

Debate tubs—slang for containers used to transport evidence

Defining—burden of the Proposition to give parameters to the resolution by giving meaning to key terms

Delay counterplans—a strategy by the opposition to simply enact the proposition's plan at a later date

Directional-focus resolution—a topic that provides some degree of direction for the debate without overlimiting the proposition team's interpretation

Disadvantage—the negative consequences of change advocated including its side effects

Effects topicality—the opposition team says that the plan itself is topical only through the effects of the government's action

Existential inherency—argument that the current situation is flawed though without identification of the problem's cause

Extra-topicality—argument that the proposition should not be allowed to advocate a plan with multiple components with elements exceeding the resolution

Eye contact—considered poor form in relation to your opponent

Fact cases—arguments focusing on contentions underlying often accepted facts

Fallacy of assumption—argument that creates a false dilemma or a misplaced blame

Fallacy of equivocation—false argument from a slight change of definitions of key terms

Fallacy of the general rule—reasoning from that which is generally true to all possible cases

Fallacy of the red herring—raising an issue that has nothing to do with debate topic

Fallacy of tradition—false argument relying on the need to maintain status quo

False cause—error made by treating correlation as cause

False dichotomy—error made when the argument limits the options to only two and ignores other possibilities

Filtering mechanism—a type of decision rule; how the arguments are to be evaluated by the critic in the debate

Gestures—body movements meant to emphasize words

Government—antiquated term used for the Proposition team

Government critiques—an alternative framework proposed by the opposition team that challenges the government mechanism in the debate

Hasty generalization—generalization made from too few examples

Heckling—practice of jeering a speaker in parliamentary debate

Impacts—magnitude of the value of action

Induction—reasoning from specific example to general class

Inherency—stock issue referring to a barrier that keeps a harm from being solved

Judging paradigm—mindset of judge who favors certain arguments and styles in decisions

Language critiques—when the opposition team argues that the proposition team should lose the debate for inappropriate or offensive language in the debate

Leader of the opposition—first speaker in critique of the proposition's position

Link—the connection of the abstract or metaphorical to the real

Metaphor—a figure of speech used to represent something else

Metaphoric resolution—resolution worded to allow creative interpretation

Movement counterplans—opposition offers a social movement as an alternative to the proposition action

Mutual exclusivity—idea that counterplans must be completely separate from plans

NDT—National Debate Tournament, one of the oldest policy-debate tournaments

Net beneficiality—argument that a plan or counterplan does more good than harm

Non sequitur—a conclusion that does not follow from the premises presented

Nontopicality—assertion that argument made by opponent is beyond the scope of the resolution

NPDA—National Parliamentary Debate Association

Opposition—squad designated in competition with the Proposition composed of a Leader, or first speaker, and a Member, the second speaker

Opposition block—segment of debate where the Member of the Opposition and the Leader of the Opposition speak back to back

Permutation—the proposition team tests the counterplan's competition by advocating both the plan and the counterplan together

Pitch—register or range of the voice in high or low tones

Plan—solution offered by proposition in answer to problem defined in the debate

Plan-inclusive counterplans—a counterplan presented by the opposition incorporating some elements of the proposition's plan

Point not taken—negative response from judge in answer to points raised in a round

Point of clarification—asked by debater in need of help to understand argument or to understand the case presented

Point taken under consideration—response from judge to allow round to continue while decision on point is made

Point well taken—response from judge accepting point raised by debater

Point of information—request made by one debater during another's speaking time

Points of order—questions raised by a debater believing that a rule has been broken by the other team

Points of personal privilege—usually question raised by debater regarding the environment of the debate or a personal discomfort

Policy cases—common extension of fact or value resolutions to allow plans of action

Prep time—time given to prepare for the debate after receiving the resolution

Prime Minister—reference to the leader of the Proposition

Rebuttal—speech designed to refute arguments made during the constructive speeches

Reductive fallacy—oversimplification that occurs when the debater does not clearly articulate the links in the argument

Significance—level of harm presented to substantiate problem

Social critiques—opposition team offers a philosophical position that counters the proposition team's framework

Solvency—question regarding whether the plan solves the problem defined

Speed—rate or pace of speaking

Squirrels—unusual definitions, plans, or cases

Straight resolutions—topics with clear parameters

Structural inherency—laws or other barriers that interfere with the plan

Subtopicality—when the opposition team states that the proposition team is addressing only part of the resolution in their interpretation of the topic

Tabula rasa—judging philosophy of the open slate where the judge expresses no preferences

Tautology—that which proves what is obvious

Topicality—demonstration that the case meets the parameters of the resolution

Topics—subjects for resolutions presented in literal or metaphorical formats

Truism—accepted fact that is unbeatable

Uniqueness—key element of disadvantages to demonstrate harm in plan

Value cases—debate comparing conflicting values

Volume—loudness or softness of voice

CPSIA information can be obtained
at www.ICGtesting.com
Printed in the USA
LVOW03s0602171217
559975LV00004B/15/P